WARRIORS
IN UNIFORM

BATTLE OF PEA RIDGE,
ARKANSAS, MARCH 7–8, 1862

WARRIORS

IN UNIFORM

BY HERMAN J. VIOLA

FOREWORD BY CARSON WALKS OVER ICE

NATIONAL GEOGRAPHIC

WASHINGTON, D.C.

OUR ENEMIES ARE CRYING

Isshe'ele Uuwateesh Iiweek
The Ones with Metal on the Top of the Head (the Lakota) are crying
Ikku'pe Uuwateesh Iiweek
The Metal Hats (the Germans of World War I and II) are crying
Chee'tbachee Pu'mmeesh Iiweek
The Short Wolf Men (the Asians of World War II, Korea, and Vietnam) are crying
Ishbi'tchia Lu'sshiash Iiweek
The Curved Knives (the Arabs of the Gulf War, Lebanon, Afghanistan, and Iraq) are crying
Alawachee' Waatcha'achik Huuash Iiweek
We heard that he was an outstanding man (the enemy soldier) but he is crying

—Crow Nation Warrior Song

FOREWORD

My name is Carson Walks Over Ice, and I am a member of the Crow Nation of Montana. My Indian name, Buffalo Chief, was given to me by my clan uncle. All the Crows have a second name in addition to their legal name. You get it from your clan uncle. The name is not for anything that you've done; it is whatever the clan uncle did and wants to give you. My clan uncle gave me his name, Buffalo Chief.

When you give away your name, you need to get another one. It is important to have a second name because the Great Spirit will not know you if you do not have a name. For example, my father-in-law came to me because he had no name. He had given his second name to a grandchild, so he needed a new name and asked me for one. He was afraid that if he died, he wouldn't be known in the spirit world. Because I was in the Army and wore a military patch with an eagle on my shoulder, I gave him the name Eagle Soldier.

I got my second name, Buffalo Chief, when I was in high school because my grandmother thought it was time for me to have another name before I left for the Army. When I was just a little boy, my second name was Flies Through the Clouds. My grandfather was wounded in the Second World War, and the Army brought him back on an airplane that flew through the clouds, so that's how I got that name. I later gave that name to my second son.

I grew up hearing war stories, but in a different way from most people in America. When I was a little guy, my grandfather George Hogan would invite people to his house to tell stories. In those days, we didn't have things like televisions—even radios—so our entertainment was stories about the old days before life on reservations. We would bring people into our homes to tell stories. We would hear about the Crow scouts who helped the cavalry like at the Battle of the Little Bighorn. We would hear the old warriors tell how they fought the Sioux, the Black Feet, and the Shoshone. They would tell us their war deeds, how they stole horses from the other tribes. For example, my grandfather's second name was Along the Hillside, and his honor song says how he went to an enemy lodge and cut a horse from out front and took it away.

All of those stories of war deeds came down to me, and my relatives would say, "This is what your dad did, this is what your uncles did, this is what your brothers did. All of them went to war and they did all of these war deeds." So when it came my time to serve, I joined. Even though I am afraid of heights, I joined the 101st Airborne Ranger Division, the "Screaming Eagles," and became a paratrooper. I was able to jump out of airplanes and helicopters, to land and attack enemy camps. I did all these things for almost ten months before I got wounded and was taken out. But when I came back from Vietnam, I could say to the other veterans, "I did all the stuff that our forefathers did, that you did, that my dad, my uncles, my grandfathers did. I did those things, too."

The Crow, like all our Native American brethren, honor their veterans. Today, when a Crow soldier returns from Iraq or Afghanistan, the family hosts a welcome home ceremony at the Billings (Montana) Airport (see page 180). The family members paint their faces and sing an honor song to the returned warrior, who is given a feathered war bonnet as part of the ceremony. Each family has its own special way of painting their faces. In the old days a special honor song was only for returning wounded warriors. The warriors, who were brought back into camp on horseback at sunrise, were serenaded with this song, which praised their strength compared with the weakness of their enemies.

The Crow Tribe has recently revived this ceremony, which is called Welcoming the Warrior Back Into Camp. A special song is now used to honor all Crow soldiers returning from Iraq and Afghanistan, whether wounded or not. This is done to encourage them and to show them that their family respects and appreciates the sacrifices they have made for their country and their people.

Before the present conflicts in Iraq and Afghanistan, the last time the Welcoming the Warrior Back Into Camp ceremony was performed was in 1970 when Eddie Little Light and I returned home from Vietnam. Both of us had been wounded. The ceremony was performed during Crow Fair (an annual gathering and celebration in Montana). Our faces were painted and we were wearing eagle feather war bonnets and buckskins. As we were led into camp on horseback at sunrise, we were followed by friends and relatives, including our mothers and grandmothers, wearing special clothes. Many people witnessed this moving and beautiful ceremony.

Although I had received numerous citations from the U.S. Army for my combat service in Vietnam, I valued more the honors accorded me by my Crow people for upholding our tribe's warrior tradition. In Vietnam I had done my war deeds. I had counted coup on the enemy.

To the Crow people, a war deed is something that says you are a man, that you have faced the enemy. It says that you have heard the gunfire and that you went and did a brave deed in front of the enemy—you are a warrior. We call these war deeds coups. If you accomplish a war deed, we say you have counted *coup* on the enemy. I guess it comes from the French phrase *coup d'etat,* "to strike."

To become a Crow chief you have to accomplish four different coups. One is to touch an enemy in battle without hurting him—you just reach out and touch him and let him go. The second one is to take an enemy's weapon away from him in battle, again doing it without hurting him. The third coup is to lead a successful war party. This means you have accomplished your objective without any of your men getting hurt. The fourth coup is to cut a horse from in front of an enemy lodge. When you do those four things you are held up in esteem in front of your people. As a paratrooper in Vietnam, I counted many coups.

Counting coup is not about killing the enemy; it is about demonstrating bravery, like the time I reached out and grabbed a Viet Cong soldier who was rushing past me through heavy brush trying to escape from a firefight. As he went past me, I reached out and grabbed him and then said, "Go" in Vietnamese. He just looked at me real funny, and then he ran. I can tell you he was one surprised fellow.

In another fight I pulled a Viet Cong soldier's weapon out of his hands. It was a Russian-made SKS carbine, and I used it the rest of my time in Vietnam. I grabbed the carbine and told him to go, so he ran and he ran.

"Why didn't you kill him?" the white soldiers with me asked. "I had my reasons," I told them, "but you saw me do it and that's all that matters."

My third deed, leading a successful war party, I accomplished many times. My war parties were the endless patrols—search and destroy missions—we conducted in Vietnam. As a platoon leader, I led a bunch of those patrols and did not lose a single soldier, but it was impossible for me to capture an enemy horse because the Viet Cong did not have any. Instead of horses they had elephants, and I did capture four of those.

It was early in the war and the North Vietnamese sometimes used elephants to carry supplies into South Vietnam along the Ho Chi Minh Trail. I was sitting on a ridge overlooking the trail one day when a Viet Cong supply column came along. It was led by a young boy. I didn't realize he was young because he was wearing a helmet and carried an AK-47. After I shot him I spotted these elephants behind him. I grabbed the rope of the lead elephant, but he kept moving. He dragged me for about 100 yards before he finally stopped. The only reason that elephant stopped was that he decided to stop. I had nothing to do with it, but when he stopped I wrapped his rope around a tree. Since he was tied to three other elephants, I can say I captured those four elephants. But they weren't horses, so the old people at home did not count them.

Because of my own combat experiences, I have been anxious to help tell the story of all Indians who have served in our country's armed forces. The telling of that story has been long overdue, and that is why I welcomed the opportunity to help with this book. Their military contributions, their sacrifices to help preserve American democracy deserve recognition. They are the forgotten heroes in this country's history. Few non-Indians are even aware that Native American men and women have served in the ranks of the U.S. military in every one of our nation's wars including our present conflicts in Iraq and Afghanistan. The sad reality is that most of these soldiers, who have come from every tribe in this country, have been "invisible."

What is even more shameful is that American Indians were not citizens of the United States until after World War I. These brave American Indian men and women went into harm's way without ever receiving appropriate recognition for their selfless contributions and service except from their own people.

Even after they obtained citizenship in 1924, Native American men and women may have been welcomed as soldiers on our nation's battlefields, but they remained second-class citizens in their own country regardless of the fact that many of them bled and died on those battlefields. Despite past injustices, our young men and women still choose to enlist and serve their country in numbers that exceed the percentage of any other ethnic group in America because we love this country.

About the only Indians who have received recognition for their contributions to our armed forces are the "code talkers." These are the Native Americans from several tribes whose unique language skills were used to such good effect by the U. S. armed forces during World War I and II and Korea. The Indians could talk to each other using codes no one outside their tribes could understand. The Japanese so feared the code talkers that their soldiers were ordered to kill them instead of capturing them.

During the Vietnam War numerous non-natives went to Canada to avoid military service because the draft was still in effect. However, I am proud to point out that many Canadian Indians came to the United States and enlisted in the U.S. Army and fought in Vietnam alongside American soldiers. I am sorry to say that these Native American volunteers from Canada have never been recognized for their contributions to the U.S. Army.

We Native Americans who have enlisted and served this country are extremely proud of our service, our sacrifices, and our accomplishments in time of war. Some of us came back uninjured, some came back wounded in mind or body, and some did not make it back at all.

—*Carson Walks Over Ice*
Crow Nation, Montana

TWO FIRES

JOSEPH BRANT, CHIEF OF
THE MOHAWK, WAS ALSO
A BRITISH MILITARY
OFFICER DURING THE
AMERICAN REVOLUTION.

Thayeadanegea
Joseph Brant
the Mohawk Chief

ntil the issue was finally resolved by the Civil War, America's Native peoples frequently found themselves caught between "two fires." During the American Revolution Indian loyalty was pulled between England and the colonies. During the War of 1812, the choice was between England and the United States. In the Civil War, it was between North and South. Nonetheless, much as the tribes would have preferred to remain neutral in these conflicts, they were drawn into the fray, and for the most part these conflicts became their own civil wars, splitting tribes as well as families. As a result, Indians have fought in every war our country has fought.

The die was cast during the American Revolution. Both sides initially sought neutrality from Indian tribes. It was not concern for Indian welfare that prompted this attitude, but awareness that they did not fight according to the rules of "civilized" warfare. Neither side wished to tarnish its image in the parlors of Europe by being the first to enlist "savages" in its armies.

Such scruples soon gave way to the necessities of this hard-fought conflict, with most tribes remaining loyal to the crown. The Indian choice was simple and pragmatic: Most of their trade goods came from England, whereas most trespassers on their hunting grounds were colonists. The fact that the Continental Congress offered the Delaware Indians their own state after the Revolution in return for their support indicates the desperation of the colonial cause. This offer, which the Delaware rejected, resembled a clause in a treaty with the Cherokees allowing them to send a representative to Congress. Neither option was likely to be accepted by the American public.

The tribes that became most directly involved in the American Revolution were the members of the Iroquois Confederacy. Powerful and primarily pro-British, the confederacy occupied a strategic location along the Hudson River between New England and the middle colonies. Of the six tribes in the confederacy, the Seneca, Mohawk, Cayuga, and Onondaga sided with the British; only the Oneida and Tuscarora took up the patriot cause.

George Washington, for one, recognized the need for Indian soldiers. They could "be made of excellent use as scouts and light troops," he informed the Continental Congress. Accordingly, the Congress in 1776 authorized him to enlist 2,000. Eventually, of the 250,000 men who served in Washington's army, about 5,500 were Indians.

A number of the Indians who rallied to the patriot cause were descendants of the so-called Praying Indians of New England, whose communities dated from the 17th century and the proselytizing activities of the Puritan missionary John Eliot. Now fully

RECALLED ONE WHITE COMRADE, THE ONEIDA "FOUGHT LIKE BULL DOGS."

assimilated and intermarried with their white and black neighbors, they little resembled their Mahican, Wappinger, and other tribal ancestors in appearance or culture.

Of these Christian Indians, the residents of Stockbridge, Massachusetts, stand out. Known as the Stockbridge Indians after their mission village located in the Berkshire Mountains of Massachusetts, the members of this Christian community were primarily Mahican, but it included other Native peoples from across New England. The Stockbridge Indians not only used their influence to keep other tribes from supporting the British, but they also formed a company in the colonial army and fought in every major campaign in the eastern theater of the American Revolution from Bunker Hill to the Battle of Monmouth.

Their effectiveness as a fighting unit ended in August 1778 when the Stockbridge company encountered a unit of the Queen's Rangers, mounted dragoons, near White Plains, New York. Although they were heavily outnumbered, the Indians fought gallantly, but were no match for the horsemen who ran them down, killing or disabling some 40 of the Mahican patriots and capturing 10. After the battle, local residents

The George III peace medal was distributed by the British to tribal leaders for loyalty and service.

buried the slain Stockbridge soldiers, including their chief, in a site now known as Indian Field in Van Cortlandt Park in the Bronx, New York.

The Oneida Indians also paid a steep price for their loyalty to the patriot cause. Like the Praying Indians, the Oneida were Christian, espousing the Presbyterian tenets of their beloved missionary Samuel Kirkland, a New England Puritan and ardent patriot. As early as 1775, the Oneida had organized their own militia company under Captain Tewahangaraghken, or Honyery Doxtator. According to his pension file in the National Archives, he organized a company of Oneida Indians "who were friendly to the Americans in their struggle for liberty, and entered the military service of the Revolutionary War."

At his side was his wife, Tyonajanegen who, at the Battle of Oriskany Creek, not only handled her own musket but also loaded her husband's gun for him after a ball wounded his right wrist. Recalled one white comrade, the Oneida "fought like Bull dogs."

Oriskany was one of the bloodiest battles of the American Revolution. Hundreds of soldiers in the patriot ranks died that day. The battle also was a major factor in the

A 1778 depiction of a Stockbridge Indian. The Stockbridge fought
in every major campaign in the eastern theater of the American Revolution.

WARRIORS IN UNIFORM

THIS PRINT DEPICTS
FIGHTING DURING THE
BATTLE OF ORISKANY
CREEK, ONE OF
THE BLOODIEST
ENGAGEMENTS OF THE
AMERICAN REVOLUTION.

CHAPTER 1

ONE ONEIDA FIGHTING WITH THE AMERICANS WAS CAPTURED BY HIS OWN BROTHER.

◆————⟨●⟩————◆

breakup of the Iroquois Confederacy because it pitted some 60 Oneidas against an equal force of Mohawks and Senecas led by Mohawk leader Joseph Brant, who held a commission in the British Army.

As a result of Oneida support for the patriot cause, the American Revolution became a civil war for Iroquois as well as colonial families. One Oneida fighting with the Americans was captured by his own brother, a supporter of the British, who then turned him over to the Seneca for execution.

Although the Indians had little effect on the military outcome of the American Revolution, their participation produced two far-reaching emotional and psychological consequences that shaped white attitudes and U.S. government policy for decades. One was a reputation for brutality inspired by the atrocities that are inevitable in every war. The other was the notion that the Indians deserved punishment for siding with the British even though several tribes cast their lot with the colonies. To make matters worse for the Indians, no matter which side eastern tribes chose, the newly formed United States did not make any distinction.

During the War of 1812, when the United States fought its second war of independence from England, tribal America again followed diverging courses. On the northern frontier, some Indians rallied to the vision of the Shawnee leader Tecumseh, who called for the tribes to unite against the United States. Tecumseh, a general in the British Army, died for his cause at the Battle of the Thames, during fighting in the Northwest.

In the South, the once powerful Creek Nation became so divided over allegiances between the United States and England that a civil war erupted between "Red Sticks" and "White Sticks." The breakup of tribal groups in the South presaged the sort of bitter fratricide that occurred during the Civil War as members of the so-called Five Civilized Tribes joined opposing forces.

Eventually, Andrew Jackson, with the aid of a Cherokee regiment and the support of the Choctaw led by Chief Pushmataha defeated the Red Sticks at the Battle of Horseshoe Bend in Alabama. Old Hickory then turned his attention to the British. Again drawing upon Indian allies, including 500 Choctaws, he attacked Pensacola, Florida. Later, at the Battle of New Orleans, Jackson's Choctaw allies led by Chief Pushmataha, buttressed his left flank.

Pushmataha, who died on Christmas Eve 1824, while on a visit to Washington, D.C., was rewarded for his loyalty to the United States with a state funeral. His dying wish—to "let the big guns be fired over me"—was honored by the Marine Corps under the direction of the secretary of the Navy and two companies of the District of Columbia militia. Two thousand congressmen, government officials, and citizens followed the cortege to Congressional Cemetery. The minute guns that thundered on Capitol Hill were echoed by three crisp musket volleys at graveside as the United States paid tribute to the Choctaw general.

No such ceremony honored Maj. David Moniac, who was killed at the Battle of

Wahoo Swamp in 1836 during the Second Seminole War. Moniac is considered by many to be the first Native American to graduate from the U.S. Military Academy at West Point. Although a couple of other cadets could claim that distinction because of mixed ancestry, Moniac is the first cadet identified as such in surviving academy records.

Referred to as the Indian Boy by academy superintendent Sylvanus Thayer, the 15-year-old Creek youngster was admitted in 1817 under the terms of a 1790 treaty between the U.S. government and the Creek Nation. A secret codicil to that treaty provided that the U.S. government would bear the educational expenses for four Creek men, and the tribe selected David to

A German portrait of Shawnee leader Tecumseh, a general in the British Army during the War of 1812. Tecumseh died October 5, 1813, at the Battle of the Thames.

Charles Bird King painted this portrait of Choctaw chief Pusmataha during the chief's visit to Washington, D.C., in 1824. The chief died soon after and was buried in Congressional Cemetery.

attend the academy. Even though Cadet Moniac spent an extra year at the academy in hopes of improving his class standing, he ranked only 39th out of 40 when he graduated on July 1, 1822. Then, after serving only about six months as a brevet second lieutenant in the Sixth Infantry Regiment, Moniac resigned his commission because of family problems back home. His decision was probably also eased somewhat by the suggestion of President James Madison that excess officers retire to civilian life, where they could impart the benefits of their West Point training to their state militias. Moniac did enlist in the Alabama state militia, as a private, but he had more success as a farmer raising cotton and breeding horses.

Ironically, even though he was married to a cousin of the Seminole leader Osceola, Moniac agreed to join the fight against his Seminole kinsmen and in August 1836 was commissioned as a captain in the Mounted Creek Volunteers. With the Second Seminole War going badly, the federal government promised the Creek volunteers "the pay and emoluments and equipment of soldiers in the Army of the United States and such plunder as they may take from the Seminoles" for their service. Moniac was the only Indian among the 13 officers who commanded the regiment's 750 Creek volunteers. The Creeks, who wore white turbans to distinguish themselves from their kinsmen, earned their money because the Seminoles were virtually unbeatable in their swampy homeland.

After leading an attack against a strong Seminole encampment near Tampa, Florida, in October 1836 Moniac was promoted to major, but his budding military career ended abruptly a month later. Part of a combined force consisting of the Creek Volunteers, Tennessee Volunteers, and Florida militia, Moniac pressed the attack against a group of Seminoles hiding in a cypress swamp behind a stream connecting two lakes. When the Creek dragoons hesitated, fearing the narrow stream was too deep to wade across, Moniac lifted his sword and plunged forward. The hidden Seminoles riddled him with numerous bullets. A witness to his death later wrote, "Major Moniac, an educated Creek warrior, in attempting to cross the creek, fell dead and the Seminoles were elated."

This lithograph depicts South Carolina soldiers along the Withlacoochee River during the Second Seminole War, which lasted from 1835 to 1842.

Osceola, one of the militant leaders in the Second Seminole War, was captured in violation of a truce and died in prison only a few days after George Catlin had painted this striking portrait in 1837.

WARRIORS IN UNIFORM

Gen. Ulysses S. Grant is shown with Ely S. Parker (seated at right), a Seneca who became Grant's secretary and achieved the rank of brigadier general during the Civil War.

On Moniac's tombstone is engraved a quote by Gen. Thomas Sydney Jesup, commander of all U.S. troops in the Second Seminole War: "David Moniac was as brave as any man who has drawn a sword and faced the enemy." Perhaps a more appropriate epitaph—one that would serve for most warriors in uniform—was written by historian Kenneth L. Benton: "He died as he lived, in two worlds: as a Major in the service of the United States Army—and as an Indian warrior in the service of his people."

Another prominent Indian soldier in this period was Ely S. Parker, a New York Seneca chief who fought for the North during the Civil War. Parker became Gen. Ulysses S. Grant's secretary and achieved the rank of brigadier general. After the war, he became the first Native American to head the Bureau of Indian Affairs, the government agency that has controlled the destiny of the nation's Native peoples since its establishment in 1824.

Parker was educated at a Baptist mission school and later studied law, but was denied admittance to the New York Bar because, as an Indian, he was not an American citizen. He then studied civil engineering at Rensselaer Polytechnic Institute. When the Civil War broke out, Parker offered his services as an army engineer but was refused a commission by both the governor

UNION ARMY COMMANDERS REGARDED INDIANS AS AN ENEMY TO BE FOUGHT.

of New York and Secretary of War Edwin Stanton, again because of his Indian heritage. The Civil War, Stanton explained to Parker, was a personal affair between white men, and he would do well to return home and tend his farm. Parker ignored this patronizing advice and continued to press for a commission, becoming a captain of engineers in 1863. Because of an earlier friendship with General Grant, he was assigned to his staff.

As in the previous North American conflicts, the combatants welcomed Indians into their armies. Indeed, American Indians fought fiercely for both sides in the war. As historian Laurence Hauptman points out in his important study *Between Two Fires,* many fought because they believed it was their last best hope to halt the genocide that had begun on the East Coast, continued through the Trail of Tears westward through the 1830s, and then exploded after the Gold Rush of 1849. But, as Hauptman points out, "the Civil War, rather than the last best hope, proved to be the final nail in the coffin in Indian efforts to stop the tide of American expansion."

As many as 20,000 Indians contributed to Union and Confederate forces both on land and on sea. They were present at most of the major battles and participated in the heaviest fighting of the war, including Second Bull Run, Antietam, the Wilderness, Spotsylvania, Cold Harbor, and the Union assaults on Petersburg. It was Parker, Grant's secretary, who drew up the articles of Robert E. Lee's surrender at Appomattox, while the last Confederate general to lay down his arms—

two months after Lee—was Stand Watie, the Cherokee commander of the Indian regiments fighting in the western theater.

For the Confederacy, Indian manpower was especially important, and southern agents actively sought Native American allies, especially among the Five Civilized Tribes—the Cherokee, Chickasaw, Choctaw, Creek, and Seminole—all of them former slave-holding peoples, despite the fact that slave-holding practices and attitudes among them varied. That these tribes joined the Confederacy was perhaps inevitable because the land they occupied adjoined Confederate states and many of their mixed-blood leaders were slaveholders sympathetic to the southern cause.

Moreover, the Confederate states offered them equal status in the Confederate government. The tribes could send representatives to the Confederate Congress and had the right to tax merchants and traders within their boundaries. The Confederate government also promised the tribes compensation for damages caused by intruders during the war.

As a result of Confederate inducements, the five tribes formally joined the Confederacy and more than 15,000 uniformed Indian soldiers fought for the southern cause, primarily in the western theater with Pea Ridge in Arkansas their most significant battle.

Perhaps as many as 4,000 Indians fought for the North. Some served in the infantry, others were scouts and sharpshooters. The Indian volunteers wore their uniforms as proudly as their white comrades-in-arms did,

A group of Cherokee Confederate veterans gather for a reunion in 1901 in North Carolina. Chickasaw, Choctaw, Creek, and Seminole also sided with the Confederacy during the Civil War.

and they suffered the same horrendous casualty rates as their white compatriots in this unbelievably brutal and bloody war. For example, of the 135 Oneida volunteers from Wisconsin in the Union Army, only 55 returned home, a mortality rate of nearly 41 percent.

Parker and a few other Indians received commissions in the Union Army and were recognized for their contributions to the war effort, but such cases were rare. If the truth be told, Union Army commanders regarded Indians as an enemy to be fought, not as warriors to be welcomed in their ranks. Had it not been for the early recruitment of Indians by the Confederacy, it is unlikely that the Union Army would have enlisted any Indians at all. Indeed, as early as July 1861, Brig. Gen. Albert Pike had succeeded in raising a regiment of Creek tribal members in the Indian Territory for Confederate service. By November the South had filled four complete Indian regiments.

DELAWARE INDIANS REST AFTER A RECONNAISSANCE MISSION ON BEHALF OF THE UNION ARMY DURING THE CIVIL WAR.

"IT IS NOT THE POLICY ... TO FIGHT HIGH-TONED SOUTHERN GENTLEMEN WITH INDIANS."

On the Union side, the War Department, as well as the professional officer corps in general, opposed the recruitment of Indian troops. Besides concern about the reliability of Indian soldiers, there was concern that they would not fight according to the rules and standards taught at West Point. As one Union officer reportedly said, "it is not the policy of our government to fight high-toned southern gentlemen, with Indians." The officer corps also believed that their lack of discipline and training would make Indians ineffectual soldiers.

Nonetheless, in the spring of 1862 the secretary of the interior formally requested President Lincoln to authorize several regiments of Indians to be recruited from refugees driven from Indian Territory by their pro-Confederate brethren.

Although Lincoln and his Cabinet concluded that neither Indian nor Negro units could be enlisted under the provision authorizing the enlistment of volunteer troops, they did agree to create a "Home Guard" of loyal Indians for local service. The secretary of war was then directed to enlist two or more Indian regiments in the Department of the Missouri. Although the Indians were to be a Home Guard, their obvious objective would be the recovery of lost homes and lands, and therefore it would be a case of Indians fighting Indians.

The formation of the Home Guard regiments almost did not occur, because the local Union commander simply forbade it. In fact, he threatened to arrest any officer who recruited Indians. At this strategic moment the former Department of Kansas was reestablished, and the new commander ordered that the Indian regiments be formed as quickly as possible.

The first military expedition, consisting of two Creek and Cherokee regiments, five white regiments, and two artillery batteries, was launched soon afterward. This expedition set the pattern of subsequent Indian participation in the war, which consisted of a series of expeditions into Indian Territory to restore the refugee Indians to their homes, neutralize the Confederate Indian force, and establish a base of operations to strike at the Confederate forces in the West. The Indians performed so well that the War Department not only relaxed its objections to their use but even looked into making them eligible for the draft as the manpower demands of the Civil War mushroomed. The inquiry got no further than the Department of the Interior, which pointed out that Indians were not citizens and thus could not be drafted.

The original objections of Union officers to Indian soldiers appeared well founded after the Battle of Pea Ridge, Arkansas, in March 1862, when some of the Union dead had obviously been scalped. Further evidence of scalping was found among both the Confederate and Union dead the following September, after the Battle of Newtonia, Missouri. This was one of the few battles of the Civil War in which significant numbers of Indians fought on both sides. These discoveries concerned both Union and Confederate commanders, who thereafter refrained from making use of Indian soldiers outside of the Indian Territory.

Of more concern, however, was the lack of discipline and military deportment of the

Thomas Bigford of Taycheeda, Wisconsin, a recruiter and farmer, swears in two Native American soldiers to fight with the Union Army during the Civil War.

LEE SAID, "I AM GLAD TO SEE ONE REAL AMERICAN…." PARKER REPLIED, "SIR, WE ARE ALL AMERICANS."

Indian soldiers, but what could the professional officer corps expect? Hastily recruited and put into battle, the Indian soldier had little time to learn the white man's military methods and codes, even had he been so inclined. Accustomed to individual, guerrilla-type warfare, the Indian soldiers preferred to fight from behind trees and rocks. Also disconcerting to white commanders was the Indian soldier's general ignorance of English, which made it difficult to execute oral or written commands, his disdain for routine camp duties, and his lack of concern about the proper cleanliness and care of his uniform. Most distressing was the Indian soldier's inclination to wander off on occasion. Regulations about unauthorized absences, one of the cornerstones of military discipline, meant little to Indian soldiers who often came and went as they pleased. Desertion was also common since the Indian soldiers usually had no loyalties to cause other than reclaiming or protecting their homes and lands. When, for example, the first Home Guard expedition into Indian Territory captured the Cherokee capital of Tahlequah, an entire regiment of Confederate Indians deserted to the Union side.

Regardless of what some officers may have thought about warriors in uniform, General Grant obviously valued the services of Ely Parker. When Grant needed someone to draft a congratulatory letter to his army after its victory at Chattanooga, he gave the task to Parker because "he was good at that sort of thing." At Appomattox Court House, Grant assigned him the task of transcribing the articles of surrender because, as one of the Union officers admitted, Parker's handwriting was so much better than anyone else's."

Robert E. Lee at first seemed taken aback at the dark-skinned Parker, when Grant introduced the Confederate general to his staff. Perhaps he thought that Grant was making a point by having a black soldier present at the surrender ceremony before realizing that Parker was a Native American. While shaking Parker's hand Lee said, "I am glad to see one real American here." To which Parker replied, "Sir, we are all Americans."

Cherokee Stand Watie commanded the last Confederate combat unit of the Civil War.

Seneca Chief Ely Samuel Parker served the Union cause with distinction during the Civil War. Later he became the first Native American to serve as commissioner of Indian affairs.

Warriors began wearing military uniforms during the colonial wars of empire when the European powers began contesting each other for control of North America. Native friendship and manpower were especially important to France and England. As a result, these countries went to great lengths to gain Native loyalty and allegiance.

An essential component of their diplomatic efforts was the presentation of gifts of state that conveyed power and authority to the recipients. These gifts included flags, silver medals, uniforms, and weapons such as swords, tomahawks, and guns. The weapons often were engraved and personalized like the tomahawk shown here that was presented to Tecumseh, the Shawnee leader, by his British patrons during the War of 1812. The inscription reads, "To Chief Tecumseh from Col Proctor MDCCCXII."

The most important diplomatic gifts were medals and flags. These carried the full weight of national allegiance and conferred upon the recipients added status and rank within their tribes. All the colonial powers, including Russia, gave such gifts to tribal leaders.

By 1789 the custom had become so fixed that the newly established United States had no choice but to continue the practice. Thus, beginning with the presidential administration of George Washington, the young republic continued to give tribal leaders diplomatic gifts in order to gain their friendship and loyalty.

Known as peace medals because many of them bore symbols of friendship such as clasped hands on the obverse, the American medals were solid silver and featured the likeness of the incumbent President. With the exception of John Adams, each President from George Washington to Benjamin Harrison issued peace medals to Indian leaders.

On this page is the portrait of Red Jacket, the Seneca chief, painted by American portraitist Charles Bird King. Red Jacket is proudly wearing the friendship medal he received from President George Washington. The medal is in the custody of the Buffalo and Erie County Historical Society.

The medals for the Washington Administration were made by silversmiths, but later they were designed and manufactured by the U.S. Mint. The first minted medals, beginning with the administration of Thomas Jefferson, came in three sizes, but later two sizes were made. The largest medals, about three inches in diameter, were presented with much pomp and ceremony to head chiefs, and the smaller medals went to chiefs and warriors of lesser rank.

A Charles Bird King portrait shows Seneca chief Red Jacket wearing his Washington peace medal.

TOMAHAWK PRESENTED TO SHAWNEE LEADER TECUMSEH, WHO FOUGHT ON BEHALF OF THE BRITISH DURING THE WAR OF 1812

To Chief Tecumseh
From Col. Proctor
MDCCCXII

U. S. Apache Scouts.

A GROUP OF APACHE SCOUTS POSE WITH THEIR INTERPRETER (FAR LEFT) AND COMMANDING OFFICER (FAR RIGHT) IN ARIZONA IN 1882.

OGLALA SIOUX WARRIOR
NO FLESH IN A STUDIO
ALBUMEN PORTRAIT
TAKEN CA 1890

When the guns of the Civil War finally fell silent, the U.S. Army underwent a dramatic drop in manpower. Authorized strength fell from 57,000 in 1867 to half that a decade later and then averaged 26,000 until the war with Spain at century's end. Effective strength, however, always fell short of authorized strength caused by high rates of sickness and desertion, so the Army was hard-pressed to provide the command and control necessary to maintain order and safety across the Far West.

Although this was an era of international peace for the United States, on the domestic front it was far different. The years following the Civil War witnessed a dramatic increase in violence across the West as various Indian tribes lashed out at the tide of white settlement that poured across the Mississippi River after Appomattox.

Faced with the realities of a shrinking Army and a huge territory to patrol and pacify, military forces in the West, both professional and volunteer, increasingly came to make use of friendly Indians in their conflicts with the hostiles. Some of the arrangements with these Indian allies were informal, with captured horses, weapons, and other booty the only payment necessary for their services. In other situations, however, the Indians were enlisted into formally organized and officered militia units just as was the case with volunteer troops by Confederate and Union forces during the Civil War. As a result, the concept of the Indian as the enemy slowly gave way to the realization that in western warfare the Indian could be an invaluable ally against other Indians.

Recognizing this, Congress in 1866 authorized the Army to enlist up to 1,000 Indians "to act as scouts…[and to] receive the pay and allowances of cavalry soldiers." Although seldom more than a third that number were in the ranks over the next three decades, the door had been opened to permit American Indians to serve as enlisted personnel in the U.S. Army. The scouts served six-month tours of duty with the option to reenlist if they wished. Many did so, forming a core group of enlistees who played important roles in campaigns against hostile Indians across the West until the era of the Indian wars drew to a close at the end of the 19th century.

For many of the Indians who served as Army scouts and auxiliaries, it was often their introduction to white culture, their first significant exposure to white ways of thinking and doing things. In fact, some of the professional officer corps viewed the use of Indians in this manner as a useful step in the process of assimilating these tribesmen into mainstream society.

One of the officers who believed this was John J. Pershing, who was stationed on the Pine Ridge Indian Reservation in South

Dakota in the early 1890s upon graduating from West Point.

In his autobiography, Pershing extolled the virtues of his Indian soldiers. They readily learned English and they provided a good example to other Indians. "It would have been an excellent idea," he declared, "to have formed one or two permanent regiments of…[Indians] as we had with the Negroes. Nothing would have done more to teach them loyalty to the government nor have gone further to bring them to civilized ways."

Because of his favorable experience with his warriors in uniform, Pershing—almost alone among the professional officer corps—supported the concept of separate Native units in World War I.

Church groups, humanitarians, and other reformers, however, did not share Pershing's optimism. They believed that encouraging the warrior way of life did the Indians a disservice. Indians should be encouraged to become farmers, not fighters, insisted the reformers and other white benefactors, who saw the warrior mind-set as the root cause of the "savagery" from which they hoped to rescue the Indians.

Nonetheless, when given the option, most western tribesmen welcomed the opportunity to join the Army as scouts and auxiliaries just so they could continue their warrior way of life as long as possible. Who could blame them? "A reservation is a prison," declared James Kaywaykla. As a child he had been one of the band members

U.S. Cavalry Company B, made up of Lakota Sioux, poses with its commander, Lt. John J. Pershing, on the Pine Ridge Agency in South Dakota in 1891.

"OURS WAS A RACE OF FIGHTING MEN—WAR WAS OUR OCCUPATION."

under Mimbres Apache raider Victorio. "Ours was a race of fighting men—war was our occupation," he boasted. "A rifle was our most cherished possession...there was not a man [on the reservation] who did not envy the scout with his rifle."

Little wonder, then, that men who regarded warfare as honorable and horses and weapons as the tools of manhood should find Army service attractive. Moreover, as soldiers, their adjustment to the white way of life was less drastic, enabling them to meet their inevitable future somewhat on their own terms. Several tribes—notably the Tonkawa, the Warm Springs of Oregon, the Pawnee, the Wyoming Shoshone, and the Crow—maintained long-term relationships with the Army.

For the Crow Nation that relationship was dictated by the harsh realities of life on the northern Plains after the Civil War as various tribes fought with each other as well as with white settlers over an ever shrinking land base. The Crow, whose traditional homeland encompassed a vast area that stretched across much of present-day Wyoming and Montana, were surrounded by several numerically superior and militant tribes including the Sioux, the Cheyenne, and the Blackfoot. Constant warfare with these traditional enemies made the Crow a brave and hardy people. It also helped explain why they allied themselves with the U.S. Army: Its enemies—the Sioux and Cheyenne—were also their enemies.

The violence on the northern Plains escalated when the federal government opened a route in 1864 linking the Oregon Trail to the gold fields of Montana. Known as the Bozeman Trail, the road passed through pristine hunting grounds that belonged to the Crow but that were also coveted by the Sioux and Cheyenne, who immediately attacked any white travelers they encountered. To protect travelers, the U.S. Army built a string of three forts along the trail—Phil Kearny, C. F. Smith, and Reno.

The posts had minimal garrisons and no Indian scouts, although 50 had been authorized. The Crow offered to provide 250 warriors to help protect the forts, but commander C. F. Carrington turned them down. He claimed he lacked the authority to enlist them as well as the weapons needed to equip them. As a result, the posts endured months of siege conditions orchestrated by Red Cloud, the brilliant Oglala leader.

Fort Phil Kearny, Carrington's headquarters, sustained more Indian attacks than any other post in American history, culminating in the destruction on December 21, 1866, of more than half his garrison in the Fetterman Fight. Crow Indian scouts doubtless would have alerted the garrison to the massive ambush that awaited Capt. William J. Fetterman and his 80 troopers.

Although never given any official status, the Crow remained in the area of the Bozeman outposts until the Army abandoned them in 1868. Had it not been for their presence, Fort C. F. Smith, which was even more isolated than Fort Phil Kearny, might have fared just as badly, but it was more centrally

WARRIORS IN UNIFORM

IN AN 1876 ENGRAVING,
SIOUX AND CHEYENNE
WARRIORS CHARGE
TROOPS LED BY GEN.
GEORGE CROOK AT THE
BATTLE OF THE ROSEBUD.

"THERE IS NOT ONE REDEEMING TRAIT ABOUT THE CHARACTER OF ANY INDIAN, LIVING OR DEAD."

located in Crow country, and the Sioux and Cheyenne had no desire to tangle with them.

In truth, the local military commanders did not trust the Crow and therefore took little stock of their advice and warnings. Typical of the attitudes of the professional soldiers at these posts is a series of newspaper articles by Lt. George Palmer, who was stationed at Fort C. F. Smith. Shortly after his arrival, Palmer wrote: "There is not one redeeming trait about the character of any Indian, living or dead." A few months later he conceded that Indian troubles were sometimes the fault of corrupt government officials. Later, after befriending some Crows and spending time with them and sharing a meal in their lodges, he gave grudging admiration to their warrior qualities, declaring that "no other Indians are braver or better fighters than the Crows." By then, the change in attitude was too late to save the posts, which Red Cloud burned after the Army vacated them.

Having learned a bitter lesson along the Bozeman Trail, the Army ten years later made ample use of Indian auxiliaries in the campaign to force Sitting Bull, Crazy Horse, and their defiant followers onto the Great Sioux Reservation.

Medicine Crow led a force of warriors fighting for Gen. George Crook as allies, not scouts.

In the spring of 1876, the Army sent three columns of troops to converge upon and trap the last free-roaming Indians, who were thought to be somewhere in the Bighorn Country. One column, under Gen. George Crook, marched northward from Fort Fetterman on the Upper North Platte River. A second column, headed by Col. John Gibbon, moved eastward from Fort Ellis in Montana. A third column, led by Gen. Alfred Terry with the Seventh Cavalry commanded by Lt. Col. George Armstrong Custer, ventured west from Fort Lincoln in the Dakota Territory.

Crook, a major proponent of employing Indian allies to fight Indians and who later successfully employed Apache soldiers to fight hostile Apaches, dispatched emissaries to the Crow Agency near Livingston, Montana, requesting the aid of Crow warriors in the campaign against the Sioux and Cheyenne. The Crow authorized a force of 176 warriors led by chiefs Medicine Crow and Plenty Coups to join Crook, but as fighting allies and not merely as noncombatant scouts. With Crook were also a number of Shoshone under the leadership of Chief Washakie.

Participants in the Battle of the Little Bighorn, including White Man Runs Him (second from left), pose in 1926 on the 50th anniversary of the battle at a monument to those who fought.

Thanks to his Indian auxiliaries Crook was saved from the fate that befell Custer a few days later. A large force of Sioux and Cheyenne led by Crazy Horse almost caught the troopers by surprise as they prepared breakfast along the banks of the Rosebud River. The subsequent Battle of the Rosebud, fought June 17, 1876, saw fighting between the Lakota and Cheyenne and the Crow and Shoshone.

According to the Indian combatants, the soldiers were just there, and sometimes they were in the way. Although there were few casualties on either side, Crook's troopers expended so much ammunition in the six-hour fight that he retreated after Crazy Horse's

followers returned to their camp along the Little Bighorn River.

Unaware of Crook's defeat, Terry and Gibbon met at the junction of the Rosebud and Yellowstone Rivers without encountering any Indians. Upon receiving word that scouts had spotted a fresh trail heading toward the Little Bighorn, Terry sent Custer and the Seventh Cavalry south along the Rosebud in hopes of finding Sitting Bull's camp. Once he found it, Custer was to block the Indian retreat into the Bighorn Mountains and await reinforcements.

With Custer were 47 Indian scouts—a few dozen Arikara, four Sioux married to Arikara

"Custer's Last Rally," a monumental oil on canvas by John Mulvany completed in 1881, captures the romantic image that prevailed of the 1876 battle between followers of Sitting Bull and the Seventh Cavalry.

women, and six Crows. One of the Crow scouts was White Man Runs Him, whose grandson Joseph Medicine Crow (see Chapter 4) was to earn his war honors as an infantryman fighting the Germans in World War II. Custer admired his Crow scouts, describing them in a letter to his wife, Libby, as "magnificent looking men, so much handsomer and more Indian-like than any we have ever seen, and so jolly and sportive; nothing of the gloomy, silent Redman about them." Indians had heard that Custer was tough, that he never abandoned a trail, and that when his food ran out he would eat mule. "That was the

WARRIORS IN UNIFORM

kind of man they wanted to fight under; they were willing to eat mule, too."

Custer may have admired his Crow scouts, but he failed to heed their advice. As White Man Runs Him later told his grandson, the Crow scouts succeeded in finding Sitting Bull's camp, but they also warned Custer that the enemy force was too large for the Seventh Cavalry to handle and advised him to await the promised reinforcements. Custer refused, lest Sitting Bull escape and deprive him of the victory he so desperately wanted and anticipated. Upon learning that Son of the Morning Star, the Crow name for Custer, planned an immediate attack, the scouts began removing their uniforms and putting on traditional fighting regalia. "What are they doing?" Custer asked Mitch Bouyer, his chief of scouts. When Bouyer repeated the question to the scouts, one of them pointed his finger at Custer and said in Crow: "Tell this man he's crazy! He is no good. Tell him that in a very

Custer's favorite scout, Bloody Knife, who was killed at the Battle of
the Little Bighorn, is shown scouting during the Yellowstone Expedition of 1873.

WARRIORS IN UNIFORM

Chiricahua prisoners including Geronimo
(first row, third from right) are photographed outside their railroad car in Arizona.

short time we are all going to walk a path we never walked before. When we meet the Great Spirit, we want to be dressed as Crow warriors not as white men!" Upon hearing this, Custer ordered the Crow scouts to leave. "I don't want that defeatist attitude around my soldiers," he told Bouyer. "We'll do the fighting if they are so afraid of the Sioux." That is why none of the Crow scouts died that day, although three Arikara were killed, including Custer's favorite scout, Bloody Knife.

The disaster at Little Bighorn could have been averted if Custer had heeded the advice of his Crow scouts. An example of this is provided by the Apache scouts who helped the Army against their hostile kinsmen. By the 1880s, of all the tribes that had once roamed freely over the American West, only a few Apache bands still resisted reservation life. Given the reservation allotted to them, Apache hostility is not difficult to understand. As part of an ongoing consolidation program, the Bureau of Indian Affairs assigned all the various Apache bands to San Carlos, a large reservation west of the Rio Grande along the Gila River. Of all the

Geronimo (left center) in a meeting with Gen. George Crook (far right) agreed to surrender two months after a raid on the Apache camp in the Sierra Madre. Two nights later he changed his mind and fled.

godforsaken pieces of landscape upon which the federal government placed Indians, San Carlos was one of the worst. "There was nothing but cactus, rattlesnakes, heat, rocks, and insects," recalled one of the Apaches who lived there. "No game, no edible plants. Many, many of our people died of starvation."

Although most of the Apaches did their best to adjust to life there, two important and effective leaders refused. One was Victorio of the Mimbres, who took to the warpath when the government refused his requests to leave San Carlos. For a year his warriors raided unchecked across Texas, New Mexico, and northern Mexico, attacking isolated ranches and travelers with American and Mexican troopers constantly at his heels.

The end came on October 15, 1880, when Tarahumara Indian scouts led Mexican soldiers to Victorio's hidden camp in the Chihuahua foothills known as Tres Castillos. Unable to escape, the Apaches fought desperately, at times fighting hand to hand. Of the 150 or so Apaches in the camp, 68 were captured, but there were 78 killed—one of them Victorio.

The other Apache raider of note was Geronimo of the Chiricahua. Unhappy with reservation life, always ill-tempered, but also crafty and cunning, Geronimo decided to leave San Carlos in August 1881 following a disturbance caused by the Army's attempt to arrest a medicine man preaching a new and—according to white observers—inflammatory religion. With Geronimo went some 100 men, women, and children.

49

CROOK ENLISTED FIVE COMPANIES OF CHIRICAHUA SCOUTS—"THE WILDEST I COULD GET," HE BOASTED.

A few months later he returned in dramatic fashion, killing the San Carlos police chief and forcing several hundred Chiricahuas to join him in Mexico.

The result was another Apache war that kept the Southwest in turmoil for the next five years. Wily, implacable, and tough, the Chiricahua were conquered only because the U.S. Army enlisted fellow tribesmen, conceding that only an Apache could catch an Apache. Credit for the tactic goes to Gen. George Crook, who had enjoyed considerable success fighting Apaches before his embarrassment at the Battle of the Rosebud against the Lakota and Cheyenne. Returned by the Army to the scene of his earlier success, Crook imposed military rule on San Carlos and enlisted five companies of Chiricahua scouts—"the wildest I could get," he boasted. They were tough as well as "wild"; eleven of the Medals of Honor given to Indian soldiers in the 19th century went to Apache scouts.

The Apache trademarks were stealth and surprise, easily achieved since war parties seldom numbered more than two dozen men. Typical was a raid in 1883 led by Chato, one of the more notorious Chiricahua freedom fighters. On March 21 Chato and some two dozen men crossed the border into Arizona, raided for six days, killed at least 11 people, covered more than 400 miles, lost only one man, and then slipped back into the Sierra Madre of Mexico without having been seen by any of the military units attempting to intercept him.

This time Crook and his Apache scouts took up the trail. Now, thanks to an agreement with Mexico that allowed U.S. forces permission to cross the border when in hot pursuit of Apache raiders, the international boundary no longer provided protection to the fugitives. When the scouts surprised Chato in his high mountain hideout, a lair no outsider had ever before breached, the raiders knew the old way of life was over. One by one the band leaders, including Geronimo, met with Crook and surrendered.

Crook's success was short-lived. Geronimo soon tired of life at San Carlos, and in May 1885 he broke out again, taking more than a hundred people with him, including Naiche, the Apache chief Cochise's youngest son; Chihuahua, an Apache chief; and Nana, who was married to Geronimo's sister. Once again the scouts found them hidden in the Sierra Madre and once again Geronimo met with General Crook and agreed to surrender, even though told they would have to be confined in the East for two years.

Crook hurriedly left to telegraph the good news to his superiors, while the prisoners followed at a leisurely pace toward the border. Along the way, the Apaches fell in with a whiskey peddler. The result was a change of heart on the part of Geronimo, who rushed back to the Sierra Madre with 20 men and 13 women.

This time Geronimo's behavior had disastrous consequences for his Chiricahua kinsmen. For letting him get away, Crook lost his command to Gen. Nelson Miles, who determined the strategy that finally brought the Apache wars to a conclusion. One reason the diehards had been so successful in maintaining their independence was their ability to visit relatives at San Carlos. These

Gen. Nelson Miles and his staff view the large Indian camp near Pine Ridge, South Dakota, a few days after the conflict that occurred at nearby Wounded Knee Creek on December 28, 1890.

visits provided occasional reinforcements and opportunities for rest and resupply. Miles, therefore, deported all the Chiricahua Apaches, including the scouts who had fought with the U.S. Army against their untamed kinsmen, to the Castillo de San Marcos in St. Augustine and other detention camps in Florida and Alabama. The deportation was as cruel as it was effective. The Chiricahuas were shipped by train to Florida in August 1886. Geronimo surrendered for the last time only a few weeks later.

Only once did the use of Indians to fight Indians backfire. In 1881 some Apache scouts turned on their fellow soldiers at Cibeque Creek in Arizona Territory. The mutiny resulted in the execution of three of the Apache scouts found guilty of murder and desertion in the face of the enemy.

Certainly some adjustments had to be made by officers who commanded the Indian scouts. One was to accept the importance of the supernatural in their lives. To the Indians, it was a matter of the highest importance. To many white observers, it smacked of superstition. At best, it was a nuisance; at worst, it hindered military efficiency. Some officers did recognize the importance of religious ceremonials and protective "medicine" to the Indian warrior's

Troop L of the Third U.S. Cavalry, shown standing
in front of quarters, was composed of Indians following an 1891 U.S. Army directive.

morale. George Custer allowed his Arikara scouts to perform the proper ceremonies before going into action. Scout Red Star later said, "Custer had a heart like an Indian." George Crook, who commanded a large force of Apache scouts, once authorized them to hold a war dance so they could be assured of spiritual protection before setting out on one of his campaigns.

The culmination of the assimilation program came at the end of the Indian wars, perhaps as a means of continuing Army control over Indians when the need for it was fading away. Following the Wounded Knee Massacre in December 1890, the Army tried the experiment of enlisting Indians not as short-term scouts but as soldiers serving five-year tours of duty in regular units. A directive issued in 1891 authorized changing the composition of Troop L in selected U.S. Cavalry regiments and Company I in selected U.S. infantry regiments to 55 Indian enlisted personnel for each troop. The white enlisted men in these companies were either transferred or discharged and the vacancies filled with Indians, usually from the same tribe. The idea was to help the Indians assimilate into mainstream American society while earning an income. The initial recruitment was to be limited to 1,000 men, but they counted against the authorized ceiling of

ONE WRITER SAID THE INDIAN "DOESN'T HAVE THE PATRIOTIC INSTINCTS A SOLDIER MUST HAVE."

25,000 active-duty personnel in the peace-time Army.

The program at first enjoyed remarkable success. The new recruits excelled in all facets of military deportment. An Apache company organized at Mount Vernon Barracks in Alabama from former prisoners of war proved so efficient at drill that the regimental commander placed it in a position of honor in battalion demonstrations. The Apache soldiers relished every opportunity to wear dress uniforms and demonstrate their abilities on the parade ground. Their commanding officer judged their intelligence to be far superior to that of the local citizens, especially the "sand hill tackies" who hovered around the base ridiculing the Apache soldiers.

Despite the evident success of the program, however, some officers expressed concern about employing Indians as soldiers. Indians admittedly did well on frontier duty fighting other Indians, the critics conceded, but could they perform as well quelling domestic disturbances such as labor strikes and racial disorders in urban settings? Why risk jeopardizing Army effectiveness, the critics also asked, simply to provide employment to a small percentage of America's disadvantaged population? Indeed, some said, why should "dangerous savages" receive such favored treatment? One writer to the *Army and Navy Journal* (May 16, 1891) reminded its readers that Greece, Carthage, and Rome had fallen, in part, because of their reliance on barbaric mercenaries. He predicted that the use of Indian soldiers would eventually undermine the moral fiber of America, declaring that the Indian

simply "doesn't have the patriotic instincts a soldier must have."

The critics never had to confront their worst fears because the experiment fell apart of its own accord. After the initial success, recruitment among reservation Indians faltered badly. Despite extensive efforts to attract recruits from eastern Indian schools, by the summer of 1895, the 1,000 Indian soldiers had dwindled to 67 men at Fort Sill, Oklahoma. This was Troop L of the Seventh Cavalry commanded by Capt. Hugh Scott. Most of the other Indian companies had only their white cadres. The units remained on active duty another two years, when the adjutant general reported there had been no enlistments or reenlistments in any of the units. On May 31, 1897, the Army declared the experiment a failure and discharged Scott's Troop L.

Why did the experiment fail? It was not the discipline or drill the Indian soldiers disliked; they could handle whatever the Army handed them. Rather, they objected to a system that violated cultural values such as making them cut their hair and living in framed buildings. They did not like the long-term enlistments or being stationed far away from their families. They also disliked much of the manual labor, which they called "women's work." On the part of the Army, the core of the problem may have been latent racism. Gen. O. O. Howard, the famed Civil War general and founder of Howard University, the black college in Washington, D.C., said the experiment had been doomed from its inception because of the fear that one day white soldiers would have to take orders from Indian non-commissioned officers. Twenty years after his troop of Indian soldiers had been discharged, Hugh Scott, now a general in the U.S. Army, confided to a friend that the Indian soldiers had been cheated of their success by an air of prejudice in the War Department.

Nonetheless, the experiment with all-Indian units did have positive results if integration into white society was the desired outcome. Legislation passed in 1894 prohibited aliens who could not speak, read, or write English from enlistment in the U.S. Army. The law, a reflection of the nativism of the time, was prompted by the increase in enlistments from the immigrant population that followed the economic depression of 1893. Although most Indians were not U.S. citizens, as a class they were exempt from the law because the Army was in the midst of its social experiment, in which one outcome was to teach English to Indian recruits. Ironically, the failure of the experiment with all-Indian units meant that individual Indian soldiers would be integrated into the Army, an equal-rights opportunity that eluded black soldiers until the Second World War.

After the experiment ended, most of the Indian soldiers returned to civilian status,

Sgt. W.J. McClure, a Choctaw, was a veteran of the 1898 Philippine campaign.

although a few remained on military rolls as scouts. During the Spanish-American War, some effort was made to organize all-Indian units, but none succeeded. William F. Cody, better known as Buffalo Bill, offered to organize units of Indians for service in Cuba, as did Richard Henry Pratt, the founder of the Carlisle School for Indians. Although Pratt had previously opposed the formation of all-Indian regiments because it flew in the face of his belief that Indians should be fully integrated into American society, he proposed forming a regiment of former Carlisle Indian students. What better way to demonstrate Carlisle's success in preparing Indian youth for their place in American society?

None of the proposed units were organized, but a number of Indians did enlist in Theodore Roosevelt's First Volunteer Regiment, known popularly as the Rough Riders. Most were in Troop L, recruited from the Indian Territory. Although no fan of the red man—in his book *The Winning of the West* he had written, "I would not go so far as to state that the only good Indians are dead Indians, but nine out of every ten are, and I shouldn't inquire too closely into the case of the tenth"—Roosevelt nonetheless had high praise for his Indian troopers because they displayed those martial qualities of which he was so fond. "We have a number of Indians," he wrote to Senator Henry Cabot Lodge in May 1898, "who are excellent riders and seem to be pretty good fellows." Some of the Indians among his Rough Riders were inclined toward wildness, he admitted, but pointed out that "their wildness was precisely like that of the cowboys with whom they were associated."

Although Indian soldiers also fought in the Philippines and a few saw action in the Boxer Rebellion in China, the real change in attitude about Indians serving in the U.S. armed forces did not come until the outbreak of the First World War.

Choctaw Bankston Johnson was one of Theodore Roosevelt's
First Volunteer Regiment in 1898, popularly known as the Rough Riders.

Plains Ledger Art

To Plains Indian warriors, drawing was as natural as fighting. Before paper became available the warriors expressed their artistic creativity on bone, bark, rock walls, and tanned animal hides, but once introduced to paper in the early 19th century they eagerly adopted the medium. Since the first paper products usually available to them were the large, lined accounting books kept by traders and military officers, their creations are known as ledger art even though the warrior artists used any paper products that came their way, including diaries, notebooks, Army rosters, and even business flyers. The ledger drawings, which frequently depicted the artist's war deeds, or "coups," were usually done in ink, pencil, or crayon. Shown are three such drawings from a ledger book at the Milwaukee Public Museum that belonged to Sioux warrior Red Hawk. According to a note inside the ledger, Capt. R. Miller originally "captured" the book from Red Hawk at Wounded Knee Creek, South Dakota, on January 8, 1891, days after the massacre at Wounded Knee. The majority of the 105 drawings in the book show warfare and horse capture, particularly between the Sioux and Crow, traditional enemies. In many, one or more of the protagonists are wearing military uniforms, suggesting that they were serving as Army scouts. Differences in artistic style indicate that several warriors besides Red Hawk used the ledger to record their war deeds. The captions may have been written by Captain Miller.

Kills a Crow

Shows the Feather

Pushes Crow gun to One Side

CHIPPEWA (OJIBWE)
INDIANS AND RETURNED
SOLDIERS IN WISCONSIN
POSE AT A WORLD WAR I
VICTORY CELEBRATION IN
1919 WITH THEIR INTER-
PRETER (FOREGROUND).

JAMES BLACK HAWK, A CHEROKEE, SERVED AS A FIREMAN SECOND CLASS ON THE U.S.S. *NORTH DAKOTA* DURING WORLD WAR I.

The Great War proved a watershed for America's Native peoples. They established a remarkable record of patriotism and selflessness during a conflict that they had no readily apparent reason to join or recognize. Nonetheless, they contributed to the victory beyond their tribal numbers and resources.

Several tribes even made it "their" war. Most notable was the Onondaga Nation of the once feared Iroquois Confederacy. It unilaterally declared war on Germany, citing the ill-treatment accorded tribal members performing with a Wild West show who were stranded in Berlin when hostilities began. A few weeks later the Oneida Nation followed with its own declaration of war.

Although most Indians in 1917 were not subject to the draft because they were not U.S. citizens, they enlisted in astonishing numbers. Even before the draft registration began, more than 2,000 had volunteered for the American and Canadian Armies, many of them eager to gain "war honors." All told, 17,213 Indians registered for the draft: Of these, 6,509, or 37.6 percent, were inducted, most of them as volunteers. The Passamaquoddy of Maine, one of the numerically smaller tribes in the U.S., fielded 500 volunteers, including their chief, Peter Neptune.

Perhaps more telling, only 228 of the 17,213 Indians who registered for the draft received an exemption; most of those were forced to do so because of their age. The Bureau of Indian Affairs later declared that of the 10,000 Native Americans who actually served in the Army and the 2,000 who served in the Navy, fully three out of four were volunteers.

These totals do not count Indians like George White Fox, a Crow who changed his name so he could enlist as a citizen. He served as George White on board the U.S.S. *Wyoming* in the North Atlantic during World War I, but when he returned to southern Montana the government refused to recognize his service. When White Fox died, there was no veteran's burial and no flag presented to his widow. His descendants continue to fight for his recognition.

The Indians volunteered and they fought, accumulating casualties and decorations that belied their small numbers. An estimated 5 percent of the Indian doughboys were killed or injured in the Great War compared with a 1 percent casualty rate for the entire American Expeditionary Force, which suffered a total of 50,280 killed and 95,786 wounded. Some tribal groups suffered even higher rates. An estimated 14 percent of the Pawnee soldiers in the AEF became casualties; the various Sioux groups suffered an average casualty rate of 10 percent.

The high casualty rate is not surprising, says historian Thomas A. Britten, author of *American Indians in World War I,* "given their often perilous duties as scouts, snipers, and messengers." In truth, Army officers

"WHEN AN INDIAN WENT DOWN, ANOTHER INDIAN IMMEDIATELY STEPPED TO THE FRONT."

motivated by romantic notions of Native American fighting abilities often gave their Indian soldiers the most dangerous assignments. Some Indians, in turn, accepted those assignments to prove their worth as soldiers and to live up to the unrealistic and stereotypical images of their warrior heritage. Nonetheless, some of the Indian soldiers did welcome dangerous duties as opportunities to fulfill their warrior aspirations.

Whatever their motivation, Indian doughboys did nothing to tarnish their warrior reputations. According to Maj. Tom Reilley, commander of the Third Battalion, 165th Infantry Division, "Indians were always at the front. If a battle was on, and you wanted to find the Indians, you would always find them at the front." During the Meuse-Argonne offensive, the first major test for American forces in the war, Major Reilly lost 476 of the 876 men in his battalion. "The Indians in the front ranks were thoroughly swept away," he noted in his report. "When an Indian went down, another Indian immediately stepped to the front."

Historian Brian Dippie estimates that 150 Native Americans earned medals from the United States for valor on the battlefield, while another 10 received the Croix de Guerre, France's highest military award. One decorated war hero was Chauncey Eagle Horn of South Dakota, who was killed in France. His father had fought Custer at the Battle of the Little Bighorn. Joe Young Hawk, the son of one of Custer's Arikara scouts at that battle, was wounded and taken prisoner by the Germans but later escaped

after killing three of his guards and capturing two others. Although suffering gunshot wounds to both legs, Young Hawk marched his prisoners back to American lines.

Perhaps the most brilliant record of the Indian warriors who fought in World War I belongs to Pvt. Joseph Oklahombi, a Choctaw in the 141st Infantry. His exploits rivaled those of the more famous Sgt. Alvin York. Oklahombi received the Croix de Guerre for scrambling across 200 yards of barbed-wire entanglements, wrenching a machine gun from its crew, and then using it to capture 171 German soldiers. He held the position for four days while withstanding a constant artillery barrage, including gas shells.

Approximately 600 Oklahoma Indians, mostly Choctaw and Cherokee, were assigned to the 142nd Infantry of the 36th Texas-Oklahoma National Guard Division. The 142nd saw action in France, and its soldiers were widely recognized for their contributions in battle. Four men from this unit were awarded the Croix de Guerre.

Indian soldiers performed well in many areas, but it was as messengers and scouts that they excelled. One reason for their success in this regard, it was believed, was an inherent sense of direction. White officers claimed that non-Indian scouts frequently had to consult their compasses when operating at night or in dense forests and thus exposed themselves to German snipers. Officers of the 142nd Regiment tested this theory by sending five Indian and five non-Indian soldiers out on a reconnoitering exercise. All the soldiers wore blindfolds.

The officers reported that each of the five Indians crawled to his objective, while the five non-Indians crawled in every direction but the right one.

Because of the German ability to intercept telephone communications, the Allies made frequent use of runners to convey messages. Invariably Indians were chosen for this dangerous duty because of their reputed courage and acclaimed scouting skills. One such messenger was Chester Armstrong Four Bears, a Cheyenne River Sioux, who reached regimental headquarters with his message despite heavy machine gun fire and a poison gas barrage that forced him to crawl most of the way from his front-line trench. Then, ignoring orders to report to the hospital for examination, he crept back to his unit.

Along the way he encountered an injured French messenger who was so grateful to his rescuer that he gave Four Bears the Croix de Guerre pinned to his tunic.

Some of the success of the Indian soldiers can be credited to German fear of "American savages." This fear was instilled by the "Wild West Shows" that had been popular in Europe in the decades immediately preceding the outbreak of the Great War and by the fanciful novels of Karl May, the Zane Grey of Germany. The late 19th-century author wrote a series of novels about the American West that established a deeply romantic and emotional tie to Indians that Germans cherish to this day. Adolf Hitler, a Karl May fan, regarded Indians as "red Aryans."

Choctaw soldiers in training to send coded radio and telephone transmissions during World War I were forerunners of the famed code talkers of World War II.

WARRIORS IN UNIFORM

MEMBERS OF A CHOCTAW TELEPHONE SQUAD WERE ABLE TO TRANSMIT MESSAGES IN THEIR NATIVE TONGUE, WHICH WAS AN UNEXPECTED BENEFIT TO THE U.S. ARMY.

Joseph Oklahombi, a Choctaw, was awarded
the Croix de Guerre after capturing 171 German soldiers.

Chief Plenty Coups, who had who led the Crow forces at the Battle of the Rosebud in 1876, participates in the dedication ceremonies at the Tomb of the Unknown Soldier 45 years later.

One of May's Indian heroes was an Apache chief named Winnetou. Although May described the Apache as honorable and noble, he also described at length the cruelty they inflicted on their enemies, acts that included torture and scalping. May also extolled the fighting skills of Native Americans, claiming that a warrior could throw a tomahawk with such accuracy that he could cut off the tip of an adversary's finger at a hundred paces. Concern about having to face American Indians in combat was so pervasive that the German press denied any were on the western front, while some American military officials, hoping to further demoralize their adversaries, suggested sending soldiers dressed as Indians on night patrols.

An unexpected benefit of the service of uniformed warriors was their role as messengers and telephone operators, because the Germans were unable to understand their languages. In the 142nd Regiment alone were Indians speaking 26 different languages or dialects. The idea originated with officers in that regiment who asked two Choctaw soldiers to transmit messages in their native tongue. Although the use of Native telephone operators was not widespread during World War I, Comanche, Cheyenne, Osage, and Lakota speakers are known to have transmitted messages on the battlefield. One difficulty with the novel arrangement, a precursor of the more organized and well-known Navajo code talking

DOUGHBOYS AND PROUD OF IT

The natural world is sacred in traditional Native American culture, and rock formations are considered to be especially powerful. Rock art—pictographs painted on stone, and petroglyphs, which are incised or chipped—can be found throughout the West. South-central Montana boasts one of the largest concentrations of rock art in the United States.

Two warriors from the Crow Nation, James Cooper and Clarence L. Stevens, were working on the Spear-O Ranch near Lodge Grass, Montana, on the Crow Indian Reservation, when World War I erupted. The two Native cowboys enlisted together and served in the same unit in France, the Fourth Infantry Division. It was nicknamed the Ivy division for its insignia of four ivy leaves on a diamond field symbolizing the Roman numeral IV.

Cooper was probably the artist for the panel below—the most recent of many Crow warrior biographic pieces at the Joliet archaeological site, in south-central Montana.

Both men returned to the cowboy life after the Great War. Their descendants are successful ranchers and cowhands.

This photograph was taken by Timothy P. McCleary, a professor of history at the Little Bighorn Tribal College on the Crow Reservation.

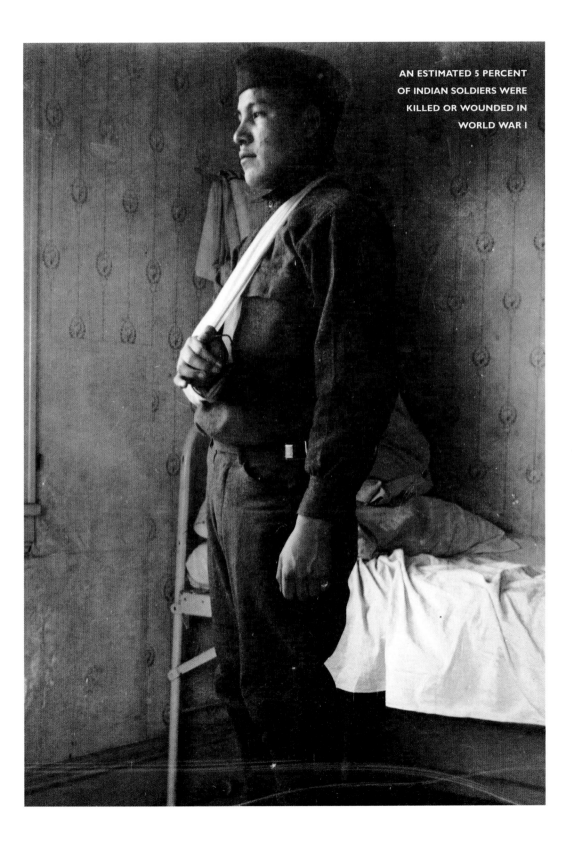

AN ESTIMATED 5 PERCENT
OF INDIAN SOLDIERS WERE
KILLED OR WOUNDED IN
WORLD WAR I

Harvier Adams, a Pima, relives a proud moment, as a member
of the 158th Infantry, 40th Division—the only all-volunteer Indian unit in World War I.

system of World War II, was the lack of military words in the Indian vocabulary. The Choctaws devised a workable code: A "big gun" meant artillery, a "tribe" was a regiment, a "grain of corn" was a battalion, a "stone" was a hand grenade, poison gas was "bad air," casualties were "scalps," and a patrol "many scouts."

Indians also contributed to the home front during the war. More than 10,000 joined the Red Cross, and they purchased more than $25 million in Liberty Bonds, an average per capita subscription of $75.

Typical of Indian support at home is the story told of a 75-year-old Ute woman who attended a Red Cross meeting on her reservation. Each finger a person held up meant a $10 donation to the Red Cross. The old woman held up five fingers, which was recorded as a gift of $50. A few days later when she limped to the agency headquarters to sign her contribution form, she became indignant when the interpreter explained she had donated $50. "I want to give $500," she declared. When the reservation superintendent told her she had only $513 to her credit on the agency account books, she smiled: "Thirteen dollars left? That's enough for me."

Perhaps it was recognition by a guilt-ridden country that thousands of noncitizen Indians had fought for the United States during World War I that accounted for the invitation to Chief Plenty Coups, who led the Crow forces at the Battle of the Rosebud, to participate in the dedication ceremonies at the Tomb of the Unknown Soldier on November 11, 1921. Whatever the reason, the choice was a good one. The Crow were traditional friends of the white man, and their warriors had fought on the side of the United States in many conflicts. Plenty Coups, acclaimed as the "Chief of all Chiefs," was 70 at the outbreak of the war and too old to enlist, but he not only encouraged his young men to volunteer—some 30 did—but he also kept a large map of France on the wall of his house so he could follow the news of the conflict. "My heart sings with pride when I think of the fighting my people, the red men of all tribes, did in this last great war," Plenty Coups told his biographer, "and if ever the hands of my own people hold the rope that keeps this country's flag high in the air, it will never come down while an Absarokee [Crow] warrior lives."

Plenty Coups was not the only Indian to participate in the formal ceremonies at Arlington Cemetery that blustery November day. One of the pallbearers was Thomas D. Saunders, a Cheyenne from Oklahoma who had received the Croix de Guerre for his exploits during the Great War. But it was Plenty Coups, dressed in full tribal regalia, who captured the attention of the 100,000 spectators. Although he was not scheduled to speak—that honor had been reserved for President Warren G. Harding—the old warrior could not resist making a few remarks as he laid a magnificent Crow war bonnet and coup stick on the casket. Lifting his arms to the heavens and speaking the Crow tongue in a voice filled with emotion, he said:

> I feel it an honor to the red man that he takes part in this great event, because it shows that the thousands of Indians who fought in the great war are appreciated by the white man. I am glad to represent all the Indians of the United States in placing on the grave of this noble warrior this coup stick and war bonnet, every eagle feather of which represents a deed of valor by my race. I hope that the Great Spirit will grant that these noble warriors have not given up their lives in vain and that there will be peace to all men hereafter. This is the Indian's hope and prayer.

WARRIORS IN UNIFORM

CHIEF PLENTY COUPS, STANDING WITH THE GROUP AT LEFT, PLACED A WREATH, HIS WAR BONNET, AND HIS COUP STICK AT THE TOMB OF THE UNKNOWN SOLDIER.

P vt. Lori Piestewa (see page 142) may well be the first female American Indian soldier ever to die in battle, although no one knows for sure.

According to *Indian Country Today,* the first active-duty Indian women were four Sioux nuns from South Dakota who served as nurses during the Spanish-American War. Originally assigned to the military hospital at Jacksonville, Florida, they were transferred to Savannah, Georgia, then sailed to Havana, Cuba, where one of them—Sister Anthony—died of pneumonia. Although given a military funeral, Sister Anthony was denied burial in Arlington National Cemetery. During World War I, 14 American Indian women joined the Army Nurse Corps. World War II saw a dramatic increase, with nearly 800 Native American women serving in a variety of capacities, but primarily as nurses. American Indian women nurses then served in mobile Army hospitals in both the Korean and Vietnam Wars.

That number has swelled dramatically since Vietnam, and American Indian women are now well represented in all of the branches of the armed forces as well as the four service academies. One of those women is Micah Rae Highwalking, a member of the Northern Cheyenne Tribe, who entered West Point in 2006. As she says:

Cadet Micah Rae Highwalking, West Point Class of 2010, at the grave of George Armstrong Custer, Class of 1861

It is a great honor for me to be representing the Northern Cheyenne people because they are marked with such respect in Indian country for their role in the Battle of Little Bighorn and the Fort Robinson Outbreak. I take great pride in going to school here even though it is sometimes awkward knowing that Custer studied in the same buildings I study in, slept in the same barracks I sleep in, and ate in the same mess hall I eat in everyday. But in the end I am comforted because I know that I am now in a position that I can help my people. As the first Northern Cheyenne to be at West Point, I'm now fighting a different war, a war that is taking my people—and all Native Americans—where they have never been. My goal is to pave the way for other Northern Cheyenne and Native American students to study at great colleges and academies. In that regard, if someone asks me if I am a warrior in uniform I say, "Yes, I am."

The Women's Memorial at Arlington Cemetery is collecting the oral histories of Native women in the armed forces.

Melinda Cain, a Pueblo-Jicarilla Apache, served as an Army specialist from 1987-90. Although celebrated as a member of the military by her male Apache kinfolk, she says her male Pueblo relatives saw the military as strictly a man's world. Melinda says that she drew on her Native traditions, such as dance, during boot camp. "The drumbeat of those songs was what I would always hear in my mind as I ran. The drumbeat kept my step in unison with everyone else and gave me strength to keep on," she told an interviewer at the opening of an exhibit associated with the Women's Memorial.

Another participant is Iva Good Voice Flute, an Oglala Sioux, who served in the Air Force from 1991 to 1995. She says that although the Air Force treated her as an equal, male veterans on the Pine Ridge Reservation did not. She recalled that while attending a powwow she was not allowed to fold the flag at evening retreat because, although a veteran, she was a woman. "I cannot forget the sting of those words," she said. "The incident changed me." Because of her efforts to change attitudes, though, the tribe has created a drum song specifically for female veterans.

Four Native American members of the Women's Army Auxiliary Corps. Several hundred Indian women served in the WACs, WAVEs, and Army Nurse Corps during World War II.

AMONG THE MARINES
RAISING THE FLAG ON
MOUNT SURIBACHI IN
1945 WAS PIMA IRA HAYES.

MEMBERS OF THE STANDING ROCK SIOUX NATION—BOTH SUN DANCERS AND UNIFORMED MILITARY PERSONNEL—SALUTE THE FLAG AT SUNRISE CEREMONIES IN LITTLE EAGLE, SOUTH DAKOTA, IN 1942.

After the Great War, Indians continued to enlist in the armed forces. At least 4,000 were in uniform in the Army, Navy, Air Force, Coast Guard, and National Guard before Pearl Harbor. Immediately upon the declaration of war, Indians rushed to enlist. Half the eligible males on some reservations volunteered for duty. Several tribes held special war councils to prepare for mobilization. The Navajo Tribal Council, for one, called a special convention in January 1942. With 50,000 tribal members in attendance the council declared its support for the war effort and promised to stand firm with the United States "until this nation shall achieve final, complete, and lasting victory."

Although as many as 45 percent of Navajo volunteers were rejected because of health and literacy requirements, some 3,600—fully 6 percent of the tribal population—served on active duty. Navajo men were so eager to join the fight some arrived at registration centers with their rifles and shotguns. At Fort Defiance, volunteers stood in the snow for hours to sign their draft cards. Nearly one-fourth of the 3,600 Ramah Navajo enlisted the day after war was declared.

The same fervor was seen throughout Indian country. One-fourth of the Mescalero Apache enlisted. At the Lac Oreilles Reservation in Wisconsin, 100 Chippewa men enlisted from a population of 1,700, and at Grand Portage nearly all the eligible Chippewa men enlisted. At Fort Peck in Montana 131 Blackfeet volunteered. Even the Hopi, whose members shared a historical suspicion of the white world, contributed 213 men, or 10 percent of their population of 2,205, to the armed forces.

A common misunderstanding among the Indian volunteers was the expectation that everyone who registered for the draft would be called into service. Many were turned down, though, for age or health reasons. "I rejected seven times on account of having old," a Pima man complained. "I am only 37 years old." Another Arizona Indian, rejected for being overweight, argued: "Don't want to run. Want to fight." A Chippewa man, rejected because he had no teeth, is said to have snarled: "I don't want to bite 'em. I just want to shoot 'em!" Also ridiculed was the idea of entering a draft lottery. "Since when has it been necessary to draw lots for a fight?" was a common joke in Indian country.

By 1942, at least 99 percent of all eligible Indian males had registered for the draft. Had all eligible American males enlisted in the same proportion as tribal people there would have been no need for the Selective Service System. The Bureau of Indian Affairs later reported that, exclusive of officers, 24,521 reservation Indians saw military service during the war. About 20,000 non-reservation Indians also served. In other words, something like 45,000 Indians, more than 10 percent of the entire estimated

ABOUT 20 PERCENT OF THE INDIAN POPULATION...
JOINED THE FIGHT AGAINST ADOLF HITLER.

population of 350,000 Indians in the United States, saw active duty in the armed forces during World War II. In some tribes, up to 70 percent of the men were in the military. And hundreds of Indian women served, as well, in the Women's Army Corps (WACs), the Navy's Women Accepted for Voluntary Emergency Service (WAVES), and the Army Nurse Corps.

All told, counting the Indians who worked in the defense industry as well as those who joined the armed forces, about 20 percent of the Indian population, or 65,000 men and women, joined the fight against Adolf Hitler, a man they called "He Who Smells His Moustache," and Benito Mussolini, who they dubbed "Gourd Chin." American Indians also invested more than $50 million in war bonds and contributed generously to the Red Cross and to relief societies for the Army and Navy. It was a remarkable show of loyalty on the part of a people who had lost almost all but their pride, dignity, and warrior spirit at the hands of the federal government.

The most celebrated of the World War II warriors in uniform were the "code talkers," Indians who communicated messages on the battlefield in their tribal languages. Building on the success of the Choctaw message transmitters of World War I, the American military made extensive use of speakers of Native languages in World War II. Although several tribes participated in the program, including Hopi, Comanche, Cherokee, and Chippewa speakers, the most celebrated and publicized were the Navajo code talkers.

John Goodluck, Sr., one of the Navajo code talkers, recalled a test conducted on the reservation for Navy officials, who were somewhat skeptical about using Indians to send secret communications. For the test, he said, the military placed radios 300 to 400 yards apart and sent coded messages using both Navajo code talkers and regular Morse code machines. "The code talkers deciphered the message in under a minute, the machines took an hour," Goodluck laughed.

Code talker messages were strings of seemingly unrelated Navajo words. The code talkers would translate each word into English and then decipher the message by using only the first letter of each English word. For example, several Navajo words could be used to represent the letter a—wol-la-chee (ant), be-la-sana (apple), and tse-nill (ax). Although the Navajo used more than one word to represent letters, about 450 common military terms had no equivalent and so had assigned code words. For example, "division" was ashih-hi (salt); "America" was Ne-he-mah (Our mother); "fighter plane" was da-he-tih-hi (hummingbird); "submarine" became besh-lo (iron fish); and "tank destroyer" was chay-da-gahi-nail-tsai-di (tortoise killer).

Eventually, 379 Navajo talkers served in the Pacific Theater. "Some say there were 400, but many failed. You had to know both English and Navajo," said Goodluck, who served in the Third Marine Division from March 1943 to December 1945 and participated in the invasions of Guadalcanal and Bougainville in the Solomon Islands; Guam; and Iwo Jima, Japan.

Code talkers from other tribes also served in the European Theater. Charles Chibitty, the last survivor of the Comanche code talkers, who died in July 2005, said two Comanche were assigned to each of the Fourth Infantry Division's three regiments. They sent coded messages from the front line to division headquarters, where other Comanche decoded the messages. Chibitty, who joined the Army in January 1941 along with 17 other Comanches, said they compiled a 100-word vocabulary of military terms during basic training at Fort Benning, Georgia. "Machine gun" became "sewing machine," Chibitty recalled, "because of the noise the sewing machine made when my mother was sewing." Since there was no Comanche word for "tank," the code talkers used their word for "turtle." "Bomber" became "pregnant airplane." "Hitler" was *posah-tai-vo,* or "crazy white man." Chibitty recalled that the first message he sent on D-Day, using the code the Comanche had created was, after translation into English: "Five miles to the right of the designated area and five miles inland the fighting is fierce and we need help."

Fortunately, despite nearly two centuries of effort, the Bureau of Indian Affairs had not yet managed to eradicate Indian languages, a fact not lost on Kevin Gover, Assistant Secretary of the Interior for Indian

Second Lt. Ernest Childers, a member of
the "Fighting 45th," received the Medal of Honor for his service in Italy.

WARRIORS IN UNIFORM

PVT. WALLACE GRANT, A
PIMA AND COMPETITIVE
RUNNER, TRANSPORTS A
MESSAGE FROM A SCOUT-
ING PATROL TO THE MAIN
LINE OF RESISTANCE IN
NEW GUINEA.

"IT'S A GREAT IRONY THAT...OUR WARRIORS WOULD PLAY SUCH A CRUCIAL ROLE IN...VICTORY"

Affairs, who spoke at a ceremony honoring the code talkers in 1999. "It's a great irony," he declared, "that in just two or three generations of being in conflict with the United States, our warriors would go forward and play such a crucial role in the victory over this country's enemies."

If the code talkers as a group were the most celebrated warriors in uniform in World War II, the best known individual was Pima Ira Hamilton Hayes, one of the

Marines who helped raise the American flag on Iwo Jima. At the age of 19, he left school to enlist in the Marine Corps. His tribal chairman told him to be an "Honorable Warrior" and bring honor upon his family. Dubbed Chief Falling Cloud at the U.S. Marine Corps parachutist school at San Diego, California, Hayes was assigned to a parachute battalion of the Fleet Marine Force upon graduation. As luck would have it, he found himself part of the American

An all-Navajo Marine Corps unit poses in Peleliu in 1944. Navajo code talkers served in the Pacific, taking part in every assault by the U.S. Marines from 1942 to 1945.

Pima Ira Hayes attended the U.S. Marine Corps
Parachutist School in San Diego, where he was dubbed Chief Falling Cloud.

Van Barfoot, a Choctaw who fought with the Fighting 45th,
was one of five Native American Medal of Honor recipients in World War II.

invasion force that attacked the Japanese stronghold of Iwo Jima. There, on February 23, 1945, he and five others—four Marines and a Navy corpsman—raised the U.S. flag atop Mount Suribachi in a dramatic moment captured for posterity by combat photographer Joe Rosenthal. Three of the flag raisers died in the continued fighting on the island, and the corpsman was wounded.

Rosenthal's photograph captured the American imagination, and, hoping to capitalize on the dramatic moment, President Harry S. Truman summoned Hayes back to the United States to aid a war bond drive.

Hayes was acclaimed an American hero, but he felt he had done nothing heroic. "How could I feel like a hero," he lamented, "when only five men in my platoon of 45 survived, when only 27 men in my company of 250 managed to escape death or injury?" Instead of being shuttled from city to city for publicity purposes, Hayes simply wanted to return to the war. "Sometimes I wish that guy had never made that picture," he confessed.

After the war, Hayes attempted to lead an anonymous life on the reservation, but it was impossible. "I kept getting hundreds of letters," he said. "And people would drive through the reservation, walk up to me and ask, 'Are you the Indian who raised the flag on Iwo Jima?'" Alcohol became his only escape. "I was sick," he explained. I guess I was about to crack up thinking about all my good buddies. They were better men than me and they're not coming back, much less back to the White House, like me."

Never married, unable to get his life back in balance, Ira Hayes died of exposure in January 1955 at the age of 32. Sadly, he died just ten weeks after attending the dedication ceremony in Washington, D.C., for the U.S. Marine Corps War Memorial, featuring the cast bronze replica of the photograph that had caused him so much pain and torment. Characterized by his Pima people as "a hero to everyone but himself," Corporal Hayes is buried in Arlington Cemetery, just a short distance away from the Iwo Jima Memorial.

Ira Hayes, like most of his American Indian comrades in arms, earned no medals for his battlefield exploits. In fact, of the 464 Medals of Honor—"for gallantry above and beyond the call of duty"—awarded to soldiers during World War II, only 5 went to Native Americans. Three of those so honored were in the same unit, the Fighting 45th: Lt. Jack Montgomery, a Cherokee; Lt. Ernest Childers, a Creek; and Lt. Van Barfoot, a Choctaw. They fought in Italy, and all three survived the war. The 45th Division was a reserve division from Oklahoma and New Mexico. Native Americans from some 50 different tribes made up the vast majority of its troops. The unit's distinctive patch bore a gold

BUT WHAT RACE SHALL I BE CALLED?

I ndians in the military in World War I were classified as white, except in the segregated South, where they were classified as "colored." Lt. Col. Mark Smith of the U.S. Military Academy, pictured at a pow-wow, wrote this poem for "those of mixed blood who are more Native in culture and thought than the race they are frequently called."

But which race shall I be called?
The recorder says: white, yellow, red, black
But I have two parents…
The recorder says: white, yellow, red, black
But my parents are from different heritage…
The recorder says: white, yellow, red, black
But which race shall I be called?
The recorder says: whichever is darker
That which is darker I am called.

WARRIORS IN UNIFORM

NAVAJO MEMBERS OF THE 158TH U.S. INFANTRY STATIONED ON THE SOLOMON ISLANDS TAKE PART IN A TRADITIONAL CEREMONY.

thunderbird on a red background in tribute to its Indian personnel. The other two Indian Medal of Honor recipients were Navy Commander Ernest Evans and Pvt. John Reese, Jr., who fought and died in the Philippines.

The actual number of Indians who served during World War II is impossible to determine because they were classified as "white" inductees, and many kept their ethnicity to themselves. In the segregated South, though, some Indians were classified as "colored" and assigned to all-black units. In fact, three members of the Rappahannock Tribe of Virginia were sentenced to six months in prison for refusing to report to a black induction station at Fort Meade, Maryland. Although they had registered for the draft as Indians, the state cited a study that concluded, "There is not a native-born Virginian claiming to be an Indian who is not mixed with Negro blood and who is not classified as Negro under the laws of this state."

Of the known Indians in the various branches of the armed forces during World War II, 550 were killed—the first one died at Pearl Harbor—and more than 700 were wounded. To those warriors in uniform, the United States awarded 71 Air Medals, 34 Distinguished Flying Crosses, 51 Silver Stars, 47 Bronze Stars, and 5 Medals of Honor.

Most of the Indians who fought and were wounded, or died on the far-flung battlefields of World War II were nameless and forgotten to the vast majority of Americans, but not to their fellow tribesmen, who honored them for their military service and often revered them afterward. This was especially true with tribes in which the warrior spirit has been predominant, such as the Crow Nation of Montana.

Andrew Bird-in-Ground was one of these unsung warrior heroes. During the Allied

Native American soldiers (left to right):
Robert Dray, Creek, Lloyd Yellowhorse, a Pawnee, and Olson Damon, a Navajo.

landing in Normandy, he earned the Bronze Star with three clusters. His Crow people felt he would have received the Medal of Honor but for the fact that he was an Indian. When Bird-in-Ground returned from the war he was given a new name, Kills Many Germans, in recognition of his battlefield bravery. Bird-in-Ground himself was very modest about his exploits. He explained that he fought so hard "because my address at the time I enlisted was in Oregon. I was afraid if I were killed in combat, they would not bury me on the Crow Reservation in Montana. I was not trying to be a hero."

He was a hero to his people, nonetheless. Shortly after returning from the war, Bird-in-Ground was visited by the worried parents of a newborn son, Kenneth Old Coyote. Kenneth, they said, was critically ill and not expected to live. They appealed to Bird-in-Ground to visit their son in the Billings Hospital and pray for him. Having survived such a terrible battle, they said, it was obvious God had blessed him, perhaps had given him special powers. Would he try to help their son? Bird-in-Ground not only visited and prayed over Kenneth, he also gave him his new name, Kills Many Germans. Twenty years later, during the Vietnam War, Kills Many Germans earned the Bronze Star himself for saving two wounded comrades while under fire.

INVARIABLY, INDIAN SOLDIERS WERE CALLED CHIEF OR GERONIMO BY WHITE COMRADES

Like the Indian doughboys of the Great War, the Native Americans who fought in the Second World War had to cope with a great deal of stereotypical attitudes and language, because most of the non-Natives they encountered had never even met an Indian before. Everything about them aroused curiosity, comment, and confusion, even their names. When Charles Kills the Enemy reported to his induction center and gave his name, he was told to get serious and give his real name. "But Kills the Enemy is my name," he tried to explain. Then there was the hospital nurse who, after checking the chart of a wounded soldier, exclaimed: "How on Earth did you get shot with two arrows?" To which he replied, "That's my name, not my injury."

Invariably, Indian soldiers were called Chief or Geronimo by white comrades. The Indians usually took no offense, since they realized the nicknames were not intended as racial insults but an acknowledgment of their reputed fighting abilities.

But of the many cultural differences between the Native and non-Native soldiers, few seemed more mysterious and impenetrable than the various purification and blessing ceremonies that were such an important part of native life. These ceremonies and the blessed objects the Indian soldiers carried, like feathers, medicine bundles, sweet grass, cedar, and other sacred objects, gave the owners peace of mind as they faced the perils of combat. Then, upon their returning home, other ceremonies purged the Indian veterans of the mental demons that often tormented non-Indian veterans. Members of numerous tribes held traditional ceremonies before going into combat. Many of these ceremonies were dances intended to weaken the enemy, such as ceremonies held on Pavavu Island after its capture from the Japanese. In one, two Oklahoma Indians slashed pictures of Hitler and Japanese Prime Minister Hideki Tojo with their knives at the end of the dance. Six Navajo code talkers also conducted a private ceremony intended to restore harmony.

Before the invasion of Okinawa, war

Lt. Woody J. Cochran, a Cherokee and a much decorated bomber pilot, holds a Japanese flag while serving in New Guinea.

"WE WERE RAISED TO BE WARRIORS BUT...EXPECTED TO SUCCEED IN THE WHITE MAN'S WORLD."

correspondent Ernie Pyle, with the Marine Corps First Division, filed a story about the unit's eight Navajo code talkers. "The Indian boys knew before we got to Okinawa that the invasion landing wasn't going to be very tough," Pyle wrote. "They were the only ones in the convoy who did know it. For one thing they saw signs and for another they used their own influence."

The "influence" was a ceremony witnessed by a "grave audience" of several thousand Marines. The face-painted Navajo Marines wore outfits fashioned from colored cloth contributed by the Red Cross and adorned with chicken feathers, sea shells, coconuts, and empty cartridge cases that jingled like bells as they danced and sang. Empty ration cans served as drums. The dancers told Pyle that they had asked "the great gods in the sky to sap the Japanese of their strength for this blitz. They put the finger of weakness on them."

The Marines did, in fact, have an easy landing on Okinawa, but things quickly got rough. "What about your little ceremony? What do you call this?" a Marine asked one of the code talkers as they hunkered down in a fox hole. "This is different," the Navajo answered with a smile. "We only prayed for an easy landing."

This was not the only ceremony performed by Native American Marines before and after the conquest of Okinawa. In a special edition of the magazine Indians at Work entitled Indians at War, mention is made of Apache, Comanche, Crow, Kiowa, Navajo, Pima, and Pueblo tribal members performing the Devil Dance, the Eagle Dance, the Hoop Dance, the War Dance, and the Mountain Chant.

In addition to conducting public ceremonies, many Indian soldiers also carried some type of personal "medicine" and credited these sacred objects with keeping them safe during the war. For instance, when Germans captured Frankie Redbone, a Kiowa, in 1944, his captors told him to put all his belongings on a table. Upon noticing a small pouch in the pile, a German guard asked what it contained. "Indian medicine," Redbone said. The guard, who probably had enjoyed Karl May's Indian novels, took everything but the pouch, and Redbone credited his medicine bundle for enabling him to survive his eight months as a prisoner of war.

The experiences of Joseph Medicine Crow can be seen as typical of Indian soldiers in the World War II era. Born on the Crow Reservation in Montana in 1913, Joseph had been raised by pre-reservation-era grandparents to be tough and strong like traditional Plains Indian warriors. "All the boys my age on the reservation were brought up in two ways at the same time," he says. "We were raised to be warriors but we were also expected to succeed in the white man's world."

The first male Crow to graduate from college—Bacone College in Oklahoma, a four-year liberal arts college with historic ties to the Native American community—and the first to obtain a master's degree, he was working on his doctorate when World War II interrupted his studies. Although offered a commission in the Army because of his academic background, Joseph turned it down on the grounds that a warrior must first prove himself on the battlefield before leading others into battle. "It was the worst

World War II Air Corps trainees at mechanic's school at Sheppard Field, Texas. Left to right: Abraham Little Beaver, Winnebago; Adam Bearcup, Sioux; Delray Echohawk, Pawnee; and David Box, Sioux.

mistake I ever made," he laughs, "because the U.S. Army didn't work on the principles of the Crow Tribe and I never got another chance at a commission. I went into the Army a private and came out a private."

Now 94, he lives with his wife Gloria in the town of Lodge Grass, Montana, on the Crow Reservation. The official historian of the Crow Tribe, he is the author of several books including *Counting Coup*, in which he describes his upbringing as a traditional warrior.

Descended from a long line of famous Crow war chiefs including White Man Runs Him and Medicine Crow, Private Medicine Crow distinguished himself on the battlefields of Germany, where he counted coup on a German soldier and even captured a herd of horses from the Waffen SS. "While serving as an infantryman in Germany," he says, "I was

able to perform the four types of war deeds, or 'coups,' a warrior needed to earn in order to become a chief." The most significant of these, he says, was to "sneak into an enemy camp at night, capture a prized horse, and then bring it back home."

The other coups, Medicine Crow explains, were: "to touch a fallen enemy, to capture a weapon from an enemy, and to lead a successful war party…one in which the goals had been achieved and all the members returned safely. To become a Crow chief, a warrior had to perform at least one of each."

When Medicine Crow went to Germany, though, he did not think in terms of counting coup. "I believed those days were gone," he says. "Naturally, however, I thought about the famous Crow warriors of the past, of my grandfather Medicine Crow who was

A two-man team of Navajo code talkers
attached to a Marine regiment relays orders over a field radio in the Pacific.

WARRIORS IN UNIFORM

Pvt. Henry Bobb, a Paiute, operates direction finding equipment for the
211th Coast Artillery at Momote Airstrip on Los Negros Island in the Admiralty Islands in 1944.

one of the most famous of our war chiefs. I knew I had a legacy to live up to. My goal was to be a good soldier, to perform honorably in combat if the occasion should occur." When he returned from Germany, though, and the elders asked him and the other Crow warriors to tell their war stories, "lo and behold—I had fulfilled the four requirements to be a chief."

Medicine Crow accomplished his first coup in January 1945, when the Allies began their push into Germany from France. "The ground was covered with snow," Medicine Crow says, and "the boundary that separated the two countries at this point was a little creek, about the size of Lodge Grass Creek, running through a canyon." The canyon was deep and had steep walls. "It was not rocky like our canyons in Montana," Medicine Crow says, "but it had real sharp hills….The French Maginot Line, with its big guns, was behind us. On the other side of this creek, facing us, was the German Siegfried line, with its big guns."

By late afternoon, Medicine Crow and his fellow soldiers had gone down the hill on the French side, crossed into Germany, and started toward the Siegfried line. "Before long," he says "we ran into foxholes just loaded with Germans," and fighting broke out. Although it soon got dark, the Americans pushed forward, with the Germans slowly withdrawing up the side of their hill toward their big guns. "As they retreated," Medicine Crow remembers, "we discovered a network of trenches higher

Pvt. Jimmy D. Benallie, a Navajo code talker with the First Marine Division, in front of a bicycle repair shop on the Island of Okinawa, April 6, 1945

WARRIORS IN UNIFORM

than your head and about three or four feet wide, going every which way. We took the main trench and followed it to the top of the hill, but it was tough going. The path was kind of steep, slushy, and muddy."

By the time Medicine Crow got to the top, about 30 or 40 soldiers who had gone before him had made the ground even more slippery. "To make matters worse," Medicine Crow says, "the guy in front of me was a fat, clumsy kid. He was always slipping and falling. When we finally reached the crest of the hill, he couldn't make it over the top. He'd get there, almost to the top, then slide down. Finally, I managed to push him up and over. Just then, the Germans opened fire, and he came sliding back down again and landed on top of me. I think that is the only reason I didn't get killed myself that day. All the guys who had gotten on top were wiped out."

The next day the division was ordered to blow up the German bunkers. "As luck would have it," Medicine Crow says, "I was standing next to the commanding officer when the message came over the telephone…. The CO said, 'Well, Chief'—he always called me chief—'I guess if anybody can get through, you can. Get six men and go up there.'"

Before he could ask for volunteers, Medicine Crow recalls, "my closest buddy stepped up and said, 'Let's go, Chief.' In all, six guys, my closest friends, went with me. I was glad only six came forward because that made seven of us, and seven is one of the numbers considered lucky by Indians."

Before the soldiers left, the company commander ordered a smoke screen. "We can't afford to let these guys go in plain sight," he said, so guns from the American side began throwing smoke screen shells on the hill to give them cover, and soon the hillside was covered with a mass of white smoke. "Then," says Medicine Crow, "we took off. We didn't know where the mines were. We just took off.

Meanwhile, the Germans realized something was happening, so they began lobbing mortar shells on us, here and there. We made it, but it took a long time crawling up that hill. It was slippery with wet snow and steep, but at least we did not set off any of the land mines."

Having arrived at the French side, the soldiers were given hot soup and coffee, and after resting briefly were told to take off again. "They gave us boxes of dynamite with fuses," Medicine Crow says. "Each box weighed 50 pounds. We tried putting them on our shoulders, but the edges cut into our shoulders, and we couldn't walk down the hill carrying them in both hands. They were just too clumsy to handle. I didn't know what to do at first. Then I just sat down, set my box on my knees, and started sliding down the hill. The other guys saw me and did the same thing. Here we were, sliding behind one another down that hill. It wasn't fast, but we made it." Meanwhile, other soldiers had thrown smoke shells on the hillside to keep it foggy, but the Germans were lobbing mortar shells and hand grenades. Medicine Crow recalls, "If our boxes had gotten hit or if we had stepped on a mine, we would have been goners. It was a terrifying experience, but somehow we all came back without a scratch and with seven boxes of dynamite. The engineers then went ahead and blew up two or three of those big bunkers."

When Medicine Crow later told this story to the elders, they told him it was the same as leading a war party. Although he hadn't come back with horses or scalps, he had returned with materials essential to the welfare of his men. "That," he says, "was my first war deed."

Medicine Crow's next war deed was counting coup on a German soldier. After enjoying leave in France, he and his unit went back into Germany. Soon after crossing the border they came to a little town, which they were ordered to enter from the rear, while other units attacked it straight on. Despite the fact that it

"THEY WANTED TO SHOOT THE GERMAN....
I FELT SO SORRY FOR HIM, I LET HIM GO."

was March, says Medicine Crow, "There was still snow on the ground. To approach the town we had to wade through a slough up to our chests. I tell you it was wet and it was cold, but it was the safest way to get into town because the Germans had planted land mines all over."

Medicine Crow and the soldiers assigned to him were told to secure a back alley in the town. With his platoon behind him, Medicine Crow began running down the alley, which, despite gunfire in the main street, was quiet. "I was carrying an M1 rifle," he says:

Along one side of the alley was a stone wall about ten feet high. As I was running, I could see a gate, so I headed for it. I wanted to see what was happening on the main street. It turned out a German soldier had the same idea. He was running towards the gate, too, but from the other side of the wall. With all the shooting going on, I could not hear him and he could not hear me either. We met at the gate. My reactions were a bit quicker than his, and I was pretty spry in those days. I hit him under the chin with the butt of my rifle and knocked him down and sent his rifle flying. He landed on his back. He tried to reach for his rifle, but I kicked it out of the way. I dropped my rifle and jumped on top of him. As I sat on his chest, I grabbed his throat and started choking him. Meanwhile, the rest of my guys caught up. They wanted to shoot the German, but I still had my hands around his throat. He was

scared. He began hollering, "Hitler Kaput! Hitler Kaput! Hitler nicht gude." He was crying. Tears were running down his face. I felt so sorry for him, I let him go.

Capturing the German counted as two war deeds. By knocking him down and touching him, Medicine Crow had counted coup on him, and he had also taken his weapon away from him, which was another coup.

The only coup that eluded Medicine Crow was also the most important: capturing a horse. The war was almost over before he managed it. "We were following a group of SS officers on horseback, about 50 of them," he explains. The officers had abandoned their men, who surrendered by the thousands. Medicine Crow and his men followed the officers all night. "They were riding their horses on an asphalt road," he says, "and we could hear the clop, clop of the hooves ahead of us. About midnight, the horsemen left the highway and went to a farm about three miles down a dirt road. We followed their trail in the moonlight and arrived at a villa with a barn and a little fenced pasture."

As the commanding officer sat down with the platoon leaders to discuss how best to handle the situation, all Medicine Crow could think about, he says, was the horses in the corral. Having decided to attack the farmhouse at daybreak, the CO started telling the platoon leaders where to take their men. Medicine spoke up, saying, "Sir, maybe I should get those horses out of the corral before you attack, because some of those SS guys might be able to escape on them. It would only take me about five minutes." The CO, he recalls, gave him a funny look, but all he said was, "OK, Chief, you're on." That was all Medicine Crow needed. As he describes it:

I took one of my buddies, and we began sneaking down towards the corral and the barn. We had to be careful in case a German was in the barn on guard duty, watching. When we got there, nothing was moving. The horses were tired, just standing around. I crawled through the corral fence and came up to one of them. I said, "Whoa. Whoa," in English. He snorted a little bit, but he quickly settled down. I had this rope with me that I used to tie my blanket. I took that rope and tied his lower jaw with a double half hitch, just like the old-time Crow warriors used to do, and then I tried to get on. But it was a tall horse, and my boots were so muddy and caked up, I had a hard time mounting. Finally, I led the horse to the watering trough and stood on that to get on its back.

Medicine Crow had told his buddy that he was going to the other end of the paddock behind the horses, and as soon as he got there he would whistle, at which point the other soldier was supposed

Three Native American women serving as Marine Corps reservists pose at Camp Lejeune, North Carolina, in 1943.

to open the gate and get out of the way. But as Medicine Crow recalls, "I got back there and whistled. Then I gave a Crow war cry, and those horses took off. There were woods about half a mile away, so I headed that way. Just about that time our boys opened fire on the farmhouse. By now it was coming daylight and I could get a good look at my horses. I had about 40 or 50 head. I was riding a sorrel with a blaze, a real nice horse. When we reached the woods and the horses started to mill around, I did something spontaneous. I sang a Crow praise song and rode around the horses. They all just looked at me."

The Germans had surrendered quickly and the firing was over, so Medicine Crow left the horses in the woods except the one he was riding and headed back to the farmhouse.

After the American soldiers had finished mopping things up and sending the prisoners to the rear, they departed down a gravel railbed. Medicine Crow, however, was still on the horse he had captured. "It was better to ride than walk," he says. "I felt good. I was a Crow warrior. My grandfathers would have been proud of me, I thought. But all too soon, the reality of the war came back. After letting me ride the horse for about a mile or so, the CO yelled over to me, 'Chief, you better get off. You make too good a target.'"

Joseph Medicine Crow's Story

In his memoir *Counting Coup,* Joe Medicine Crow describes the warrior tradition and his own response to being inducted into the Army in 1942: "In the pre-reservation days," he says, "a Crow young man aspiring to be a warrior would go into the Wolf Teeth Mountains seeking spiritual power. He believed that this power would make him a better warrior."

This experience was called "Going Without Water," was a three- or four-day total fast that was thought to encourage the appearance of emissaries of the Great Spirit. The animal spirits would ensure the vision seeker's success in battle. Some warriors added to the discomfort of the ritual by cutting off a finger. An alternative to seeking a vision was to be blessed by a veteran warrior or spiritual leader.

Medicine Crow opted not to undergo the ritual before shipping out, saying, "I preferred to do my communicating with the First Maker in church." But he did bring traditional "medicine" with him: a special feather he received from his uncle, Tom Yellowtail. Before each battle, Medicine Crow put the feather inside his helmet, recited prayers, and painted himself with a red lightning streak and red ring. "I did not put the paint on my face," he says, "but on my arms under my shirt. My uncle taught me how to paint myself properly. If I did not have paint, I could use a red pencil." It was this medicine, Medicine Crow says, that protected him despite a number of close encounters he had with the Germans.

On one occasion, Medicine Crow's company was marching when they came under artillery and mortar fire from Germans directly across a narrow valley. Despite the vulnerability of their position, Medicine Crow says, "I felt pretty well prepared. My haversack was full of pemmican my mother had sent me. I had my rifle. I had painted the symbols on my arms, and I had put the medicine feather in my helmet."

An artillery shell, though, soon exploded in front of Medicine Crow, the force of which knocked him over the side of a hill. Although he received only some bruises, he says, "It killed or wounded about a half dozen of the soldiers nearest me." His helmet, haversack, and rifle gone, Medicine Crow began the laborious task of ascending the hill. Along the way he found his rifle, and then located his haversack.

"Near the last tree at the top of the hill, he remembers, "I found my helmet with the feather still tucked in the liner. When I put the helmet back on, I came to my senses. Everything was now all right, but I admit I had panicked there for a while. I have always attributed that particular sequence of good luck to my special Indian medicine. Whenever I had a close call, I would think about that medicine," he says.

After he returned to the United States, Medicine Crow gave the feather to a fellow soldier, his cousin Henry Old Coyote, who was a machine gunner on a B-25 fighting in the European Theater and Africa.

"I think after the Second World War that feather then went to Korea with a Crow soldier," Medicine Crow says. "It might have even gone to Vietnam. I don't know where it is now, but it certainly was powerful."

JOSEPH MEDICINE CROW,
ABOUT TO ENTER THE
DANCE ARENA AT CROW
FAIR, HOLDS A DANCE
STICK REPRESENTING THE
HORSES HE CAPTURED
FROM GERMAN SS OFFI-
CERS IN WORLD WAR II.

CHAPTER 4

WOLF MEN: KOREA

A BUGLER PLAYS "TAPS"
DURING A MEMORIAL
SERVICE AT THE FIRST
MARINE CEMETERY IN
HUNGNAM, KOREA, FOR
CASUALTIES OF THE
FIGHTING IN 1950
AT CHOSIN.

MEN OF THE FIRST
MARINE DIVISION
ADVANCE THROUGH
THICK SMOKE ALONG
THE KOREAN FRONT
IN 1951.

Immediately following World War II and the Berlin Airlift of food and supplies to that conquered city in 1947-48, another war began—the Cold War. The geopolitical chess match between Russia and the United States dominated the second half of the 20th century.

The Cold War had its hot moments, notably in Korea and Vietnam (see Chapter 6), where the United States sought to prevent the anticipated expansion of communism in Southeast Asia.

Overshadowed by World War II and Vietnam, the Korean War is often referred to as the forgotten war. It began June 25, 1950, when North Korean troops crossed the 38th parallel dividing the Korean Peninsula. It featured some of the most vicious fighting and worst conditions that American soldiers had ever experienced .

But it also was marked by remarkable accomplishments, from the morale-boosting landings at Inchon and the entrapment and remarkable escape of the First Marine Division at the Chosin Reservoir to the savage hill fighting at war's end. Three years of intense fighting had caused the combat deaths of almost 37,000 Americas.

Although China—which had supplied its neighbor North Korea with supplies, ammunition, and other support—the United States, and the United Nations agreed to an armistice in 1953, South Korea refused to sign, leaving the two Koreas separate and the war in suspension to this day.

America's native peoples paid scant heed to the geopolitical implications of the Cold War. Their country needed fighting men, and they answered the call. No matter that their adversaries now were the "Short Wolf Men" of Asia instead of the "Metal Hats" of Germany, the warriors in uniform again enlisted in numbers that far exceeded their percentage of the American population. Exact figures are difficult to establish, but it is believed that 10,000 Indians served in Korea and that, of the 54,000 American fatalities reported by the Department of Defense, 194 were Indians.

One of the American Indians who served in the Korean conflict was Ben Nighthorse Campbell, a Northern Cheyenne who later became one of the few American Indians ever to serve in the U.S. Congress. A high school dropout, Campbell joined the Air Force in 1951 and spent a year in a police unit in Korea.

Like other warriors in uniform, he greatly valued his military experience. "There was a camaraderie that transcends ethnicity when you serve your country overseas in wartime," he said in the Native American newsletter *Canku Ota* (*Many Paths*). After the war, Campbell devoted his life to judo and to politics, retiring in 2004 after serving

President Harry S. Truman presents Capt. Raymond Harvey (second from left) with the Medal of Honor. Harvey, a Chickasaw, was one of four Native Americans to be so honored during Korea.

three terms as a member of the U.S. House of Representatives and then two terms as a U.S. Senator from Colorado.

Another Native serviceman who achieved renown was Joseph "Jocko" Clark. Born in Pryor Indian Territory (later Oklahoma) to a Cherokee father, Clark attended the U.S. Naval Academy in Annapolis, Maryland, and was its first Native graduate.

With the outbreak of World War I, a newly graduated Clark served aboard an armored cruiser on combat duty in the Atlantic. He went on to serve in World War II and Korea, where he would become commander of the Seventh Fleet, before retiring as a full admiral.

Also an accomplished pilot, Clark drew on his heritage in naming the Cherokee Strike, a combat maneuver he devised that aided ground forces in Korea.

Four American Indians were awarded the Medal of Honor for heroism in Korea. One was Pvt. 1st Class Charles George, a Cherokee from North Carolina who sacrificed his life by throwing himself on a hand grenade to protect his fellow soldiers.

"WHEN A MAN GOES INTO BATTLE, HE EXPECTS TO KILL OR BE KILLED AND IF HE DIES HE WILL LIVE FOREVER."

Capt. Raymond Harvey, a Chickasaw, led his platoon against entrenched positions, personally killing several of the enemy with carbine fire and hand grenades and then, although wounded, refusing to be evacuated until his company's objective had been achieved.

The third Medal of Honor recipient was Cpl. Mitchell Red Cloud, Jr., a Winnebago from Wisconsin and a veteran of World War II. Corporal Red Cloud, a member of Company E, 24th Infantry, was on a ridge guarding his company's command post when he exchanged fire with enemy troops who had launched a surprise attack. Although severely wounded, Red Cloud braced himself against a tree and continued shooting, thereby enabling his company to consolidate its position and evacuate the wounded. Corporal Red Cloud received the Medal of Honor posthumously on July 2, 1951. On the monument erected in his honor at Black River Falls, Wisconsin, is inscribed, "The son of a Winnebago chief and warriors who

Cpl. Mitchell Red Cloud, a Winnebago from Wisconsin, was awarded the Medal of Honor.

believe that when a man goes into battle, he expects to kill or be killed and if he dies he will live forever."

The award of a posthumous Medal of Honor to a fourth Native American hero of the Korean War was authorized by Congress in 2007. Known to his family and friends as "Woody" and to his fellow soldiers as "The Chief," Woodrow Wilson Keeble is only now receiving recognition for his remarkable exploits on the battlefield in World War II and Korea.

A member of the Wahpeton Sisseton Sioux Tribe of North Dakota, Sergeant Keeble was awarded five Purple Hearts, two Bronze Stars, a Silver Star, and a Distin-guished Service Cross. Twice his men recommended him for the Medal of Honor but no action was taken during his lifetime. U.S. Senators from both North and South Dakota—both states claim Keeble as a native son because the Wahpeton Sisseton Reservation straddles the state boundaries—wrote the legislation authorizing the posthumous honor.

Orphaned at the age of nine, Keeble spent most of his youth at the Wahpeton Indian Boarding School in North Dakota and returned there after his military service. An exceptional athlete, he was being recruited by the Chicago White Sox as a pitcher when he was called to service in World War II. He saw combat throughout the South Pacific with the North Dakota Army National Guard's 164th Infantry Regiment, and he had a well-earned reputation for taking care of his men. As one recalled, "The safest place to be was next to Woody." In fact, he received his first Purple Heart and first Bronze Star on Guadalcanal while attempting to rescue several fellow soldiers.

When the Korean War broke out, Keeble reenlisted. Asked why, he said, "Someone has to teach those kids how to fight." Keeble returned to service at the age of 34 as a master sergeant. And it was from the Korean War that he emerged as the most decorated military hero in North Dakota history. To his comrades in arms he demonstrated behavior "often seen in movies but seldom seen on the actual place of combat," as Sgt. Joe Sagami said in recommending that Keeble receive the Medal of Honor.

Keeble's defining moment came on October 20, 1951, during Operation Nomad, the last major U.S. offensive of the war, as his company battled Chinese communist troops near Kumsong. Two days earlier he had engaged the enemy in a firefight for which he would later receive the Silver Star. Now, although already wounded twice and suffering from a badly damaged knee, Keeble ignored requests from medics and his men to remain behind when his company was ordered to take a nearby hill. Not until they had nearly reached the top, however, did the soldiers realize that they had climbed into an inescapable trap with entrenched enemy troops directly above them. "They were throwing so many grenades at us," one of the trapped soldiers remembered, "it looked like a flock of blackbirds flying over."

Keeble took matters into his own hands. Armed only with an M-1 rifle and hand grenades, he crawled toward the enemy and waged a one-man war. Thanks to his pitching skill, he managed to destroy three machine gun bunkers with well-aimed hand grenades, killing nine Chinese and wounding the other crew members. Although hit multiple times during this assault, including by a concussion grenade that stunned him momentarily, he attacked two trenches filled with enemy troops, killing seven before the rest ran away. On the back side of the entrenchments, his soldiers found a Chinese command post, which explained why the enemy had fought so fiercely. For this exploit, Keeble received the Distinguished Service Cross.

Although he had fragmentation wounds in his chest, both arms, both thighs, right calf, and right knee, Keeble refused evacuation because no replacements were available. He returned to duty even though his wounds were bleeding through his bandages, he was limping badly, and he was so weak he could hardly lift his rifle. Little wonder that there was such a determined effort to get Sergeant Keeble the medal he so richly deserved.

Following his service in Korea, Keeble returned to the Wahpeton Indian School, where he held several positions until a series of strokes rendered him speechless and unable to work. Hard times forced him to pawn some of his medals. He died in 1982 at the age of 65 and is buried in Sisseton, South Dakota. "It's hard to believe he had the warrior-like capabilities because outside of a war setting, he was so likeable,"

"THEY WERE THROWING SO MANY GRENADES AT US, IT LOOKED LIKE A FLOCK OF BLACKBIRDS."

said Kurt Blue Dog, one of his relatives, in an article in *Indian Country* about the congressional action.

Another of the unsung heroes of the Korean War is Vernon Tsoodle, a member of the Kiowa Nation. Now living near Meers, Oklahoma, with his wife of 58 years, the Marine Corps veteran served two tours in Korea and two in Vietnam before retiring in 1973 with the rank of master gunnery sergeant (E-9) after 30 years of military service, including his time with the National Guard. He was awarded the Bronze Star for heroism during the Korean War. Like so many of the

Native Americans in the military today, he is descended from noted warriors, and his family has followed in that tradition. Including those who have married into the Tsoodle clan, the family can claim more than 30 men and women who have served in the armed forces since World War II, including his two sons, a daughter, and three grandchildren.

In addition to the influence of ancestors, Tsoodle was shaped by other forces. In 1937, at the age of six, he was taken to Riverside Indian School in Anadarko, Oklahoma, because his grandparents, who

Although twice recommended for the Medal of Honor, Master Sgt. Woodrow Wilson Keeble (far left), with members of the 24th Infantry Division near Kunsong, Korea, did not receive it in his lifetime.

Sgt. Raymond Wahkinney, a Comanche who operated a 105-mm howitzer, saw some of the bloodiest fighting of the Korean War at places like Porkchop Hill, Old Baldy, and Heartbreak Ridge.

were raising him, could barely make ends meet. The only income they had was from farming and some money they got from grazing rights.

"You hear a lot of negative things about Indian boarding schools," Tsoodle says, "but for me they were a blessing because I learned things such as discipline, which later served me well in the Marine Corps. A famous Marine general once said, 'The difference between being afraid and being helplessly frightened is discipline.' That not only applies to the Marine Corps but to life itself. If you are afraid, that's fine. If you are disciplined, you can handle any situation."

From Riverside he went to Chilocco Indian School for high school. Chilocco had a National Guard unit, but it was empty because everyone had been sent overseas to fight in World War II, so Tsoodle enlisted in the Oklahoma National Guard at the age of 14. "My rifle seemed like it was taller than I was," he remembered. Five years later he married a high school classmate, Jimmie Leah Reese. With the return of veterans from World War II, Tsoodle couldn't find a job, so he enlisted in the Marine Corps. "I had to keep my marriage a secret, however," he says, "because the Marine Corps was not accepting anyone who was married."

The discipline Tsoodle received at Riverside and Chilocco, inured him to the rigors of boot camp. "At Indian boarding school," he says, "we were taught when to eat, when to brush our teeth, when to breathe. Boot camp was a snap compared to Indian schools."

WARRIORS IN UNIFORM

After graduating from boot camp, in response to the worsening situation in Korea, Tsoodle was rushed to the peninsula. Years later he still remembered a magnificent display of firefighting over the city of Inchon when he first arrived.

In Korea Tsoodle was a communications lineman, ensuring landline communications between each unit, because radios were not always reliable. This often put him in hostile territory stringing wires. He recalled sitting at the top of a telephone pole connecting a wire when fighting broke out in a village about a half mile away. "I was mesmerized watching the firefight and Marines moving from door to door through the town," he says. "I watched for what seemed like a long time until it dawned on me that I was a sitting duck on top of

that pole and that a sniper could take me down in one second. You never saw someone scurry down a pole as quick as I did that night!"

Tsoodle wound up with the Marines trapped at the Chosin Reservoir, where 16,000 U.S. servicemen—including 12,000 Marines—faced more than 100,000 Chinese soldiers. The Chosin campaign prompted the famous Marine cry "Retreat, hell. We're attacking in a different direction."

The soldiers earned the nickname "Frozen Chosin." Tsoodle says the cold was no exaggeration:

> We did not realize how cold it was until we got up there. Temperatures of 30 and 40 degrees below zero were common. The ground was so frozen

Men from the First Marine Division march down a pier to board the U.S.S. *Henrico,* an attack transport that participated in the historic landing at Inchon, Korea, in 1950.

WARRIORS IN UNIFORM

CHAPTER 5

"I REMEMBER BEING SERVED A WONDERFUL THANKSGIVING DINNER…BUT IT FROZE SOLID."

we couldn't dig foxholes. We had to lay behind rice paddy dikes and things like that for protection. You couldn't build a fire because you would give your position away. All you could do was just lay there and endure the cold. I remember being served a wonderful Thanksgiving dinner with all the fixings but it froze solid while I was eating it. Even had there been no enemy shooting at us, we wondered how we could survive.

Having been cut off by the Chinese, members of the wire team were faced with the grim job of unloading the wounded and the dead from incoming helicopters. "Many of the dead that we unloaded were in grotesque positions," Tsoodle remembered, "because once they were killed, they froze in that position. If we saw steam coming from their noses, we knew they were still alive and we carried them over to the medics so they could triage them by determining which men would live and which men wouldn't. It was a sorrowful job but you had to do it."

Tsoodle saw frontline action when the First Marine Division was ordered to the village of Hagaru-ri to set up division headquarters. On the east side of Hagaru-ri was a vital airstrip. Tsoodle, with the First Signal Battalion, was part of the advance party to tie headquarters to the Fifth and Seventh Marine Regiments, set up north and west of Hagaru-ri at the end of the Chosin Reservoir.

Upon leaving division headquarters they began stringing their lines overhead so track vehicles like tanks wouldn't tear

them up, but just as they got to the edge of the headquarters compound, they started receiving sniper fire. Not knowing what was going on, they called the division wire officer, who ordered them to come back. Only then did they realize that they were surrounded.

With the Chinese now pressing them on all sides, Marines not assigned specific duties were formed into rifle platoons. Tsoodle's military occupation specialty was telephone communications, but he had first been trained by the Marine Corps to be an infantryman, he says, "so in situations such as this, they can take you and put you on a piece of equipment such as a machine gun, and you shouldn't have any problem operating it." The wire team was turned into a .30-caliber machine gun squad and tasked with defending the airstrip.

To reach their defensive position, they had to go up a steep incline to reach the ridge-line. "We had to re-supply ourselves with ammunition, which meant carrying M-1 bandoliers and grenades," Tsoodle says. The icy terrain made maneuvering in their winter boots difficult for the soldiers.

When it was Tsoodle's turn to make the trip, he strapped on six bandoliers of ammunition and started up the hill. "I'd make a little headway and then start losing traction so I'd take off a bandolier to lighten the load," he says. "I'd make a little more headway and slip again so I'd have to lose another bandolier. By the time I made it to the top, I was wearing only one bandolier! The next Marine in line tried to do the same thing, with the same results."

Vice Adm. Joseph J. "Jocko" Clark, a commander
of the Navy's Seventh Fleet during the Korean War,
was of Cherokee descent.

On the opposite hill, Tsoodle noticed a number of brown spots—fox holes that were dug by the Chinese. The soldiers set up their machine guns behind a rice paddy revetment and waited for the Chinese to attack.

The attack came at night. "We always knew when [the Chinese] were coming," Tsoodle says, "because they would start yelling and screaming and shooting off tracers. I can still remember the bells and whistles that signaled the Chinese to attack. The Chinese would come running down the hill with all kinds of noise makers, and they would fill the air with green incendiary or tracer rounds that ricocheted off the rice paddies all around us because the ground was so frozen."

As fighting continued, the machine gun barrels got red hot and the soldiers fired aimlessly. "You didn't even have to pick out a target," Tsoodle says "because if you shot out there, you were going to hit somebody and sure as heck, we did. When daybreak arrived, it was nothing to see hundreds of Chinese lying dead out there."

One night the Chinese decided to attack the Americans' tank park, setting off 55-gallon drums of diesel fuel. When the drums exploded, the entire sky was lit up, illuminating thousands of Chinese coming down from the hill. Tsoodle recalled that they looked like "ants whose hill had been disturbed." Because the crews slept around their tanks, they were able to react quickly and defend themselves. The next day, as they walked among the dead Chinese soldiers, the Americans could see that many of them carried only a blanket, tooth powder, a toothbrush, and a comb. Their food was grain strapped around their body, says Tsoodle, like a bandolier, and despite the extreme cold, they were wearing only tennis shoes and quilted cotton uniforms. "That was their cold weather gear," Tsoodle says. "You sure had to pity them because they were in worse shape than we were."

The UN forces succeeded in getting out, but at a terrible cost; there were something like 10,000 casualties, many of them because of the intense cold.

Tsoodle was awarded the Bronze Star with the Combat "V" (below) because he was in

PRIVATE TSOODLE'S BRONZE STAR

The Bronze Star is awarded to "any person who...distinguished himself or herself by heroic or meritorious achievement or service...in connection with military operations against an armed enemy; or while engaged in military operations involving conflict with an opposing armed force in which the United States is not a belligerent party." The citation accompanying Tsoodle's bronze star reads:

"For heroic achievement in connection with operations against an enemy while serving with a Marine signal company in Korea on 28 November 1950. Private First Class Tsoodle, acting as a machine gunner in a machine gun squad of a reinforced rifle platoon comprised of communications personnel, displayed outstanding professional skill and initiative. When his platoon was assigned the mission of reinforcing an infantry company in defense of the Hagaru-ri, Korea airstrip, he fearlessly assumed an exposed position and placed accurate and effective fire on enemy positions. Despite numerous casualties suffered by his platoon, he continued to remain in position throughout the night and by his fire, inflicted numerous casualties on the enemy. His aggressive actions were an inspiration to all members of his platoon and contributed materially to the successful defense of the airstrip. Private First Class Tsoodle's initiative and courageous actions were in keeping with the highest traditions of the United States Naval Service."

Pvt. 1st Class Vernon Tsoodle's Bronze Star had an attached V for Valor because he displayed courage under fire while serving in Korea.

"I WAS JUST A GUNG-HO
18-YEAR-OLD MARINE DOING HIS JOB."

charge of the machine gun section, which held the Chinese away from the airfield. Despite having been a participant in one of the major battles of the conflict, Tsoodle says, "In situations like that you don't realize how much peril you are in until after it's over. I was just a gung-ho 18-year-old Marine doing his job."

An inscription on the Korean War monument in Washington, D.C., says "All gave some, some gave all." Tsoodle, who considers himself "one of the lucky ones," grows emotional when he thinks of the Marines who did not make it out. "I think of them and then I wonder why, despite four combat tours—two in Korea and two in Vietnam—I never got a scratch."

And Tsoodle's luck extended to his family:

When I was getting ready to ship out of Korea, people at the debarkation port started telling me that there was a guy who looked just like me asking for me. I knew exactly who it was, my brother Thee. He was also with the Marines, and he had walked something like ten hours just to see me off. We spent my last night in Korea together and he watched me leave the next day. It was one of the hardest things I've ever had to do, leaving my brother behind and not knowing if we would ever see each other again. However, he served his time in Korea and came home safely. It was a joyous reunion when we saw each other again. We were the closest in age, so we had a special bond.

Tsoodle says that when he joined the Marines he never saw himself as an Indian:

I was a Marine. As a Marine you develop close ties with other Marines because you are together for extended periods of time, away from your homes and families and dependent on each other for survival. Our bond was common. We were no longer separated by race. We were Marines. Because I was an Indian, however, my fellow Marines throughout my career called me "Chief." People have often asked if that offended me. It didn't, and it still doesn't. It was never said or meant in a derogatory manner. To them a chief was a leader, so how could that be a bad thing to be compared to? I was pleased because a chief is a great warrior.

Another Native veteran of the Korean War is Gilbert Towner, a member of the Tututni, one of the Siletz Confederated Tribes of Oregon. One of the last speakers of the Tututni language, Towner is proud of his warrior legacy. His Indian name is Ensalun, the name of his great-grandfather, who was a war leader of the Tututni in the Rogue River Wars of Oregon. Family members of Towner's also served in World Wars I and II. Interviewed for the First Warrior Project, which has preserved the images and stories of 100 Indian veterans, Towner says, "We uphold the tradition of my great-grandfather. We are Americans."

Like his friend Vernon Tstoodle, he was one of the "Chosin Few." On the night of

Sgt. 1st Class John Rice, a Winnebago, was denied burial in his native Sioux City, Iowa, but President Truman arranged for burial with full military honors at Arlington Cemetery.

April 23, 1951, while in a foxhole atop a mountain ridgeline, Towner was shot in both legs and an arm. A fellow Marine hunkered down with him was in even worse shape. "He was losing a lot of blood," Towner says, "and could hardly raise his rifle to shoot. I figured that if he stayed there he would die from his wounds, so I decided to try to get him to the medics." Towner crawled out of the foxhole thinking he would lift the wounded soldier out, but, unable to stand, managed instead to drag him out of the hole by using his belt to tie both of the soldier's hands together and slinging the soldier's arms over his head. The two had crawled out of the foxhole a short way when they encountered

three Chinese who had broken through. "They were just sitting there, evidently exhausted or disoriented," Towner says. "I shot all three of them with my pistol and then we continued on our way down the backside of the mountain to the aid station." Towner refused treatment himself and crawled back to his position, but suffering from wounds in both legs, his arms, and his head, he had to be carried off the mountain the next morning.

A sergeant who witnessed his heroics promised to recommend Towner for a Silver Star. He did get three Purple Hearts, but the Silver Star never came. "I was new to the outfit—I came up that night—and nobody knew me," Towner explained.

"IT WAS SCARY BEING IN COMBAT, BUT I TRIED NOT TO THINK TOO MUCH ABOUT IT."

In many respects, life for him was worse after the war. Like so many soldiers, he never fully recovered physically or emotionally from the stress of combat. Unable to meet the Marine physical requirements because of his injuries, Towner took his discharge in 1958. "I just went home and tried to pick up my life where I'd left off, but I couldn't do it," he says. "I had been a logger before I joined the Marine Corps and tried to go back to the same job, but I couldn't do the work because of the wounds. Also, because of things I went through, I used to have some real bad dreams. I was in real bad shape. I drank an awful lot. I tried to use alcohol to overcome my problems, but it didn't help." For eight years Towner wandered the streets, working when he could, before reconnecting with his Indian culture. "I relied heavily on my Indian culture, using the sweat house, to straighten myself out," he says.

Towner eventually succeeded. He got married and found employment with the U.S. Postal Service, the first of a series of government jobs that would last for 25 years and enable him to earn disability retirement. Today, he still lives with the pain of his wounds, and with their consequences. In winter, the skin on his hands cracks at the joints, and he is afflicted by degenerative arthritis—the result of the severe frostbite he suffered in Korea. And like others who shared such experiences, he still suffers from those memories. Nonetheless, he says he is now content. He has been married for 20 years, has four children and five adopted stepchildren, and he is an honored member of his tribe. "I don't feel sorry for myself at all," he says. "I just thank God I'm alive and able to meet the new day."

His sentiments were echoed by Raymond "Rusty" Wahkinney, a Comanche who experienced some of the heaviest and bloodiest fighting of the war. Sergeant Wahkinney, a member of the Oklahoma National Guard who died in February 2007, also was haunted by his memories. He talked about a cold so intense that tanks could cross major rivers without breaking through the ice. He experienced combat so brutal it seemed no one would come home alive. He recalled sitting back to back with his buddy in their fox hole on the front lines during the nighttime attacks as bullets and shrapnel flew around them.

The youngsters in his command would break down and cry, sobbing that they would never see home again. "I would talk to them," he says. "I told them to pray because the Lord will take care of you. That would calm them down for a while, but then it would start all over again the next night. It was scary being in combat, but I tried not to think too much about it. I would concentrate on what I was supposed to be doing, and that was operating a 105-mm cannon."

During his three years in Korea with the 158th Field Artillery of the famed Thunderbird Division, Sergeant Wahkinney's unit fired 15,373 rounds at the North Korean and Chinese Armies as they slugged it out at Pork Chop Hill, Old Baldy, Heartbreak Ridge, and the other bloody engagements that marked the Korean War. Like other Indian servicemen, he was called "Chief." "The nickname never bothered me," he says, "because I saw myself as a warrior fighting for all Indian people as well as for my country."

Vernon Tsoodle's Story

I was born in the vicinity of Mountain View, Oklahoma, in 1931. Tsoodle (Red Teepee), my great grandfather, was the father of Satanta (White Bear), the great Kiowa warrior, and Old Man Tsoodle, my grandfather. Satanta was a member of an elite society of Kiowa warriors called Kaseenkos. Only the top ten warriors of the tribe could be members. I have been told that if that society still existed, I would be considered a member because of my war record.

Among the Kiowa people, the war record is the most important determinant of status within the tribe. From the war record flow all the great rewards of Kiowa culture. Because of my warrior lineage, I am a member of the Kiowa Gourd Clan. Its members were always the strongest and most able-bodied men of the tribe. It was their duty to protect the tribe and serve as hunters, warriors, and camp policemen.

I lived with my grandparents, Old Man Tsoodle and his wife, Kau Tompa Hodle. She was named after a skirmish at a swimming hole during which someone was killed. It was customary to give grandparents a child to raise since they had no more children of their own at home, and the grandchild would be around to help take care of them. It was also a way to ensure that tribal traditions and culture would be carried on by the next generation. Since my grandparents could not speak English, I learned to speak Kiowa. That enabled me to converse with other elders. That was one of the advantages of being raised by your grandparents because you got exposed to other elders within the tribe.

As a child, I heard many stories about Kiowa warriors from the tribal elders who visited my grandparents. For example, I learned that when our horsemen would close in on their enemies, the war chiefs would shout *"Bay-Pae-Tay! Bay-Pae-Tay!"* "Courage! Courage! Whenever I was engaged with the enemy during my tours in Korea and Vietnam, those words would race through my mind.

When WWII broke out all of my siblings enlisted almost instantly. My brother Fred joined the Army Air Corps and my brothers Hawley and Brennen and my sister Mildred joined the Navy. Their example inspired my brother Thee and me to pursue careers in the military.

My grandfather was a keeper of one of the sacred bundles of the Kiowa Tribe, the Ten Grandmothers bundle. Every day during the war he took out that bundle and prayed. He prayed not only for his grandchildren but also for all the other members of the Kiowa Tribe who were in the military and for our country's success in the war.

I don't think my grandmother fully understood what was happening, but she expressed her patriotism whenever an airplane flew over our homestead. It didn't matter what kind it was, a military plane or a commercial airliner like Braniff or TWA, as soon as she saw it she would stop what she was doing and give a loud trill called a lulu, which is a cry a Kiowa woman makes when she is proud and happy. She did it to show her pride in the fact that her grandkids were defending our country.

VERNON TSOODLE THOUGHT OF THE BATTLE CRIES OF THE KIOWA WAR CHIEFS DURING HIS TOURS IN THE MILITARY. IN 2000, HE WAS ELECTED TO THE OKLAHOMA MILITARY HALL OF FAME.

U.S. MARINES REST
IN HUE AFTER A
BATTLE DURING
THE TET OFFENSIVE.

AN AMERICAN GI,
WEAPON DRAWN,
CAUTIOUSLY MOVES OVER
A DEVASTATED HILL NEAR
FIREBASE GLADIATOR.

Of the more than 42,000 Indians who served in the military during the Vietnam era, 135 were members of the Crow Nation of Montana including Carson Walks Over Ice, a nephew of Joseph Medicine Crow (see Chapter 4). Like his uncle, Carson had grown up listening to stories about the great Crow warriors of the past, and he volunteered to go to Vietnam even though his service commitment was about to end, because he wanted to live up to the warrior traditions of his people.

Ernie Dogwolf Lovato, an Apache from Lingo, Wyoming, joined the Marines and went to Vietnam for the same reasons. In an account of his experience preserved by the American Native Press Archives and Sequoyah Research Center, Lavato admitted,

> The greatest thrill to a young man is to become a warrior and get status within the tribe. That's our ultimate goal. The sad thing about becoming a warrior these days, however, is that they're no longer counting coup. It's got to be a war. So, how do we get our young ones to be warriors without killing them?… I feel strongly that our Indian people have to learn from this war and they have to learn that being a warrior is really not as important as having a son or a daughter, and watching their sons give them children and grandchildren. There are

a lot of men [who went] there that will never know their grandchildren. I'm the fortunate one. I've got nine grandbabies.

As is evident from from the story of Carson Walks Over Ice, the warrior tradition provides a common bond, a shared brotherhood in the U.S. military, even with members of tribes that once were traditional enemies. In Vietnam, Walks Over Ice's best friend, who later became his adopted brother, was Richard Spider, a Sioux, once the mortal enemies of the Crow.

Although few in number, relatively speaking, Native American soldiers seek each other out, regardless of tribal affiliation. John Luke Flyinghorse, Sr., a Hunkpapa Lakota from McIntosh, South Dakota, another Vietnam veteran whose account is archived by the research center, tried to explain: "American Indians always looked each other up…no matter what tribe we were from. That was the only mystique…why? I have no idea, but we had a bond.…No matter where we came from, we always walked point, or carried the radio, or were the Company Commander's operator…always."

As Walks Over Ice points out, Indians were always expected to be a little bit better than their non-Indian companions. "We had a certain reputation to live up to," he says. Of course, not all Indian soldiers appreciate that pressure. In fact, many soldiers of American

Indian heritage who grow up away from traditional communities and values are dismayed to find themselves thrust into dangerous situations because the fact that they are Indian supposedly makes them "super" soldiers.

Typical is the experience of the Vietnam veteran who told Tom Holm, author of *Strong Hearts, Wounded Souls,* that whenever his unit went on patrol, his lieutenant made him walk point, which meant he was in front of the patrol looking out for ambushes and booby traps. Finally, the soldier asked his lieu-

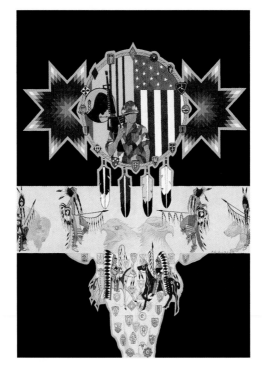

The painting "Akicita Wasté" ("Good Soldier") by Martin Red Bear combines Plains warrior symbols with military imagery.

tenant, "Why are you doing this to me?" "Well, you're an Indian," the officer replied. "You know your way around the woods." "I was born and raised in Chicago," the soldier answered.

One bond that most Native American soldiers share is a staunch belief in the spirit world. Religion is at the core of native life. Rituals and sacred objects are closely held, with few non-Natives allowed access to the secrets of the kiva, the sweat lodge, or the Sun Dance.

The Sun Dance, which is the highest religious expression of the tribes of the northern Plains including the Crow, is usually a three-day ceremony in which participants abstain from food and water while dancing and blowing a whistle made from a hollow eagle wing bone. Dancers often suffer from extremes of weather. Some collapse from hunger and exhaustion in their effort to communicate with the spirit world as they seek visions, help with personal problems, or blessings for friends and relatives.

Bobby Talks Different, a Vietnam veteran of the Gros Ventre Tribe from the Fort Belknap Reservation in northern Montana, danced eight times. "I did this to keep my promise to the One Above, he says. "Eight of us…went to Vietnam together and I promised the One Above to do a Sun Dance for each life that returned. All eight of us came back, and I thanked the One Above by undergoing eight Sun Dances. The others never knew of my vow."

The story of Carson Walks Over Ice is not unique among Native American soldiers; what is unusual is his willingness to share it. When he went to Vietnam in 1966 he took into battle two medicines—one that he wore around his neck, and one that he wore around his waist—and credits them for his courageous performance and his safe return home.

He notes of his service:

I certainly had some close calls, like the day my platoon was directed to search an area recently burned clear by napalm. When about half of my

"AS I WENT DOWN, I COULD SEE THE MUZZLE FLASHES FROM THE MACHINE GUN."

platoon was across the burned out area, I was about to step out into the open when a voice right next to me says, "Hey, there is something wrong. Watch out!" I looked around but nobody was there, so I stepped out. At once a machine gun to my right opened up. The ground around me literally exploded. As I went down, I could see the muzzle flashes from the machine gun. I began shooting. I killed the gunner, and he fell backwards.

Another guy stepped in and I shot him. Then a third guy came forward, and I shot him. As he fell, I jumped up, and at that moment a bullet tore my wristwatch off, leaving a red mark across my arm, but I didn't realize it at the time. As I ran to the right, another machine gun crew opened up on me, but again they missed and I was able to cut around to the side and kill those gunners. By then I was shaking because of the adrenaline rush. As I tried

Dewayne C. Luther, Laguna-Hopi, relaxing with one of his buddies in Vietnam. Luther served two tours in Vietnam in a special arms unit but later committed suicide after his return to civilian life.

A Vietnamese boy who often interpreted for the wiremen stands in front of a jeep known as the Mighty Might used by the 11 Marine Regiment communications platoon as a wire-laying vehicle.

to calm down, I looked at my wrist to see the time, but there was no watch. Since then I can't wear a watch. I don't know why but when I put a watch on my wrist, it stops.

In honor of his uncle, Joseph Medicine Crow, Walks Over Ice went to Vietnam hoping to return a Crow war chief like him. Also to follow in his uncle's footsteps, he sought to perform the four types of coups needed to become a Crow war chief (see Foreword); because the Viet Cong did not have horses, however, he was unable to perform one of them. He did, however, take a scalp in Vietnam. He was one of a number of Native soldiers who did and says:

I did it because that was part of Plains Indian warfare, and I saw myself as part of that warrior tradition. I took the scalp on my very first combat action in Vietnam, in September 1966. We were sent into a valley looking for a Viet Cong battalion. We were taking heavy ground fire. Our team had four helicopters, and mine was the only one that made it in. The other three were blown out of the air. As soon as I hit the ground, I ran right into an enemy soldier. He popped up out of nowhere. I shot him. He was wearing a pith helmet with a red star. As he flipped backwards, his helmet flew off and I saw he had his hair tied in a scalp lock. It was a pretty one, wrapped with beads and red flannel cloth, so I took my bayonet and cut it off. The non-Indian soldiers who later saw it would say, "Why did you do that? That is barbaric." But they would cut ears off dead Viet Cong and say, "This is my trophy." Well, that scalp was my trophy. I had counted coup on that enemy, just like my ancestors did. I kept that scalp, but I blessed it with incense from sweet grass afterwards so that no bad things would come with it. I had that scalp until I got wounded and taken to Japan.

After the war, a boy back home came to me and said, "I need a name." He was a member of my clan, the Big Lodge Clan, so I gave him the name "Takes a Pretty Scalp." Even though someone took the scalp from me after I was wounded, that name lives on among the Crow people.

Walks Over Ice brought back two other names from his tour in Vietnam, which live on among his people. He gave the name Skydancer, after the leg-kick reaction paratroopers have when their parachute snaps open, to a nephew. He named a friend's son Kills the Pretty Enemy for the four female Viet Cong machine gunners he killed during a firefight.

During the war, M16s were used by U.S. troops. Walks Over Ice used an SKS carbine, which he had captured early in the war. The M16 "was like using a .22-caliber rifle," he says. "I shot one guy 20 times and he did not drop, so I threw that M16 away and switched to the SKS." Because the SKS was Soviet make, the only way he could get ammunition was from enemies he had killed.

Because Viet Cong snipers always tried to pick off soldiers wearing leadership insignia like stripes or bars, Walks Over Ice, like the other soldiers, never wore markings on his uniform. Instead, he tucked an eagle feather in the back of the netting that covered his helmet. With the feather sticking up, the other soldiers could recognize him in the heat of combat, especially in the jungle, where it was hard to discern the enemy. On the front was printed "Chiefie," his platoon's nickname for him. "On one side I had my wife's name, Verlie," he says, "and inside I kept her picture so I could see her every day. She was my salvation [over there. She was also] the one who kept me from going off the deep end when I came back....Without her, I don't think I would have made it. She kept me from having bad dreams and all that kind of thing."

In the Vietnam War, it was Army policy not to put Indians together. In Walks Over Ice's company there were four Indians, one in each of the four platoons: He was in the first platoon, his friend Richard Spider was in the second, a Ponca in the third, and a Klamath in the fourth. "Even though we were often separated, it was great having Native soldiers nearby. Whenever we saw each other, we would say, 'hey.'

"That's a difference between Indian and non-Indian soldiers," he says. "When Indians see each other, it's like old home week. It made no difference if we were not next to each other in the field, because Indians talk with their hands, in sign language. We understand each other in sign. The non-Indian soldiers would see us doing it and say, 'What are you doing?' I'd say, 'I'm talking to him.' Even though we were 100 yards apart we could talk to each other."

As for being an Indian, Walks Over Ice felt fully accepted by his comrades. "I never noticed or experienced any discrimination, although non-Indians would look at me differently because of my name, Walks Over Ice," he says. "Most of my fellow soldiers had never met an Indian." In Walks Over Ice's experience, he and other Indians felt they

WARRIORS IN UNIFORM

AT THE ANNUAL CROW FAIR IN MONTANA, EACH DAY BEGINS WITH A PARADE THROUGH THE ENCAMPMENT LED BY A CROW HONOR GUARD FOLLOWED BY RIDERS IN TRADITIONAL REGALIA.

CHAPTER 6

had a certain reputation to live up to as Indians—that they were "a little better than everybody else, that we fought harder, that we were braver, that we were leaders."

Walks Over Ice tells of a new recruit who came up to him and said, "I am a replacement, and I want to be in your platoon." "What do you mean?" Walks Over Ice said. "You're in second platoon." "My dad was in World War II," the recruit replied, "and he said, 'If you ever get into combat, find an Indian and he will keep you alive,' so I want to be with you." "OK," Walks Over Ice said. "I'm in first; my brother Richard Spider is in second, go find him." Says Walks Over Ice: "My brother [Richard] kept him alive."

For valor under fire Walks Over Ice earned the Silver Star, the Bronze Star, and the Purple Heart. He earned the Silver Star during a search and destroy mission as part of a large American force seeking to intercept a North Vietnamese regiment going toward Cambodia and Laos. Walks Over Ice says:

We ran into the whole regiment and wiped out one entire battalion, the Fifth. To reach the enemy, we had to climb [a prominence]. It was real steep. It was almost like mountain climbing, pulling ourselves up, and we didn't see this enemy trench as we reached a long ridge leading to the top. As my point man tried to get his footing on the ridge, he got shot and flipped over me. Instinctively, I grabbed him by his web gear and then pulled myself up. I had my M16 in one hand and just blasted away, firing one-handed, until I ran out of ammunition. In the excitement of the moment, I didn't even realize that I was still carrying this guy until he moaned in my ear when I finished firing. Would you believe I later saw him on a television program?

Anyhow, I laid him down and reloaded. I killed all 15 guys in the trench. As I advanced up the ridge, I then came under fire from two machine guns. I killed the six-man crew and captured both guns. Starting out again, I ran into another machine gun emplacement. I killed that crew and then continued up the same ridge. Farther up was a .50-caliber machine gun that I captured after killing the 11-man crew. When I got on top of the ridge, 44 of the enemy were still there, including the battalion commander. They all surrendered.

Walks Over Ice was awarded the Bronze Star the following February. The objective was a suspected Viet Cong base camp. His platoon was dropped into the area following a bombing run by B-52s to sweep in and clear the area of any surviving enemy.

"As we moved forward after landing, an enemy machine gun opened up on me," he recounts, adding:

I fell and began shooting and killed all three men in the crew. I then ran over and captured the gun. As I did that, I came under fire from another machine gun to the right. The only thing that saved me is that as I jumped up the machine gun jammed. As the gunner reached over to fix it, I shot him in the head. I then saw that the two machine guns were guarding a Viet Cong camp across the river....I yelled to my men to follow me and I jumped into the river. As I splashed across someone tossed a grenade at me, but I ducked under the water and was not hurt. When I reached the other side I opened fire with the machine gun I had captured and began knocking people over. I

THE PLAINS TRADITION

Among Native tribes, war deeds have long been documented by Native artists. For the Lakota, like many of the tribal nations of the northern and southern Plains, they have been recorded in the form of ledger drawings (see pages 56-57), tepee liners and tepee covers, winter counts (calendars of events), and personal items of clothing and other personal accessories. A warrior could commission an exceptional artist to record his war deeds or he could record them himself.

"Honoring Our Lakota Vietnam Veterans" puts a contemporary spin on a Plains tradition.

I am a contemporary native artist, and in 2001 I was preparing for the Northern Plains Tribal Art Show, which is held annually in South Dakota. As I was trying to decide what to enter in the juried competition, I thought about creating a miniature or toy tepee. I considered replicating a tepee decorated with battle scenes, but eventually I decided to create a tepee honoring Lakota Vietnam veterans, and one in particular—Charles Pablo, my uncle. My uncle Charlie had served three tours of duty in Vietnam, and at one point was missing in action.

My uncle carried the Lakota name of Tagani Kopi Shi (Afraid of Nothing). After his second tour of duty, when I was a sophomore or junior in high school, he signed up to go back, and I asked him why. My uncle said he wanted to serve again so that I wouldn't have to. I didn't have to serve in Vietnam, and would watch America's involvement end on television during my freshman year in college.

My piece for the show, "Honoring Our Lakota Vietnam Veterans," consists of four dolls dressed in Army uniforms, carrying flags and weapons, with long braids and beaded moccasins. There are four female dolls dressed in a variety of the traditional Lakota dress styles. One doll is waving a feathered fan, one doll is waving a white handkerchief, another doll is waving her shawl, and one doll is simply waving the hand. These gestures are indications that a family member has performed a brave deed such as serving in the military. Accompanying this piece is a beaded toy tepee decorated with beaded helicopters, crossed American flags, and a single beaded eagle. Traditional tepees (even toy tepees) are painted to depict wartime accomplishments, such as raiding enemy horses, or battles with enemy tribes and the U.S. cavalry. I included the helicopters because I had heard that the Vietnam War was sometimes referred to as the helicopter war.

I don't believe that my uncle would say that he had accomplished any great deeds while he served in the military, but I believe that he carries on a long tradition of the Plains warrior, to guard and protect the people, which I have tried to reflect in my art.

—Emil Her Many Horses

didn't know that I was by myself over there until I had to stop and change ammunition belts for the machine gun.

Walks Over Ice got shot on his next mission. "My first stop was a hospital in the Philippines," he says. "From there I went to Okinawa, then Japan, and finally a military hospital in Denver."

The only other medal Carson thought he deserved but did not get was the Soldier's Medal, an award given for a noncombat heroism. He recounts the incident, saying:

We were at an air strip out in the middle of nowhere north of Saigon getting treated for dysentery caused by some bad water they had given us.

Our field packs were lined up in a row while the guys lined up for treatment. I was the only one in my company not sick.

C Company was to our left, and their packs were laid out, too. While they were waiting their turn someone began cooking his C-rations. The burner was nothing more than a C-ration can with a gasoline tablet in it. Well, the wind came up and knocked over that…can. The gasoline spilled onto a pack and set it on fire, causing it to blow up. Then, one by one, all of C Company's packs blew up.…The area was full of smoke. While I was in there a soldier appeared from nowhere and bumped into me. I yelled, "Get out of here!"

Shown here are tepees belonging to the Tsoodle family,
who camp together each year at the Kiowa Gourd Clan Celebration in Carnegie, Oklahoma.

WARRIORS IN UNIFORM

"OUR PEOPLE SAID, 'YOU DID SOMETHING GOOD. YOU DID SOMETHING GREAT FOR YOUR PEOPLE.'"

◆———◉———◆

As we were running, another one of C Company's packs blew up and a grenade came flying toward us....The grenade hit the kid in the leg, knocking him down and burning his pants. I didn't want to, but I ran back and picked him up. Not until I got back to the company area did I realize I had carried him the whole way. My CO put me in for the Soldier's Medal for that particular incident, but I didn't get it.

Walks Over Ice's return to the reservation coincided with the annual Crow Fair. During the fair, the tribe held a ceremony for Walks Over Ice and Eddie Little Light called "the warriors' return." It is a traditional method of honoring warriors returning safely from war. Walks Over Ice says:

At sunrise one morning the old men took us to the top of the ridge above the camp where all these teepees are. We were all on horseback. The old men then paraded us through the camp singing warrior honor songs and waking everybody up. The people then followed us into the dance arbor where we sat on our horses next to our womenfolk while the old men danced with rifles. As they danced, they sang, "This is what our men did." The dancers performed a pantomime of the deeds that each of us did in battle while an announcer described our war deeds. They told the spectators that we were defending our families, our people, and our country.

For Walks Over Ice and his fellow warriors in uniform the homecoming was different from that of the non-Indian. "Our people," Walks Over Ice recounts, "said, 'You did something good. You did something great for your people.'...The respect and honor we received helped a lot of the bad things we experienced to go away."

Despite the encouraging homecoming, the trauma of some experiences lingered. For Walks Over Ice the most traumatic was the death of his buddy Richard Spider, a Crow Creek Sioux in his company. Their last battle took place when their company was ambushed while on a search and destroy mission. Three of the four Indians in the company were hit. Spider, who was scheduled for discharge in three weeks, was killed, as was the Klamath, and Walks Over Ice's right leg was shattered. The Ponca was the only Indian left standing.

Soon after Walks Over Ice returned home, he went to visit Spider's family at Fort Thompson in South Dakota and, as part of the Indian tradition of replacing a lost loved one, was adopted by them. Remembering that time, Walks Over Ice says:

Richard's dad was a Presbyterian minister. He took me as his son because we had served together, his boy and me, and I named my middle son Richard because of him. Richard was a good man. He was older than I was. He got the Bronze Star and a Purple Heart....He was a good soldier. For some reason, he knew he was going to die and I was going to make it....He's not here and I am, but his name lives on with my son.

The Power of Medicine

Our warrior beliefs come down to us in stories. I'm descended from a line of Crow chiefs. My great-grandfather fought in the Indian wars. My grandfather was in the First World War. My dad was in World War II. My uncle was in Korea. Growing up, I was taught that joining the military was how you became a warrior, how you show your pride in being a Crow. The warriors in our tribe dance to their honor songs. The little boys listen to their war stories. As a little boy you say to yourself, I can do the same thing. One day I will go to war and defend our people.

In the old days, Crow warriors defended their people and their land from enemy tribes, but now that the intertribal war days are over we have to go into the military in order to do our warrior deeds. Even though the Crow people have suffered much at the hands of the United States government, we accept the responsibility to fight the enemies of our country instead of enemy tribes. I could have gone to Canada like the white boys who were afraid to fight, but no, it was my turn. I knew I had to go to Vietnam because of the warrior traditions in my family and my tribe. Besides, I wanted to count coup, to do my war deeds. The only way I could do that was to go to Vietnam and be part of the action. I volunteered to go, unlike the other guys who flew with me to Vietnam. Everyone else on that plane had been drafted.

However, I felt I had an advantage over the non-Native soldiers in Vietnam because of my Indian heritage. The spirit world is very important to us and it is hard to find anyone who does not believe in the "One Above," the creator. Native spiritual powers protected me and gave me peace of mind. For example, while in Vietnam I carried two powerful "medicines." One was a medal with wings on it from my grandmother that I wore around my neck. The other one was made for me by a Crow medicine woman. I wore it on a string around my waist. I lost both of them in one fight. They were shot off. A bullet came through my shirt and ripped away the medal hanging around my neck; another bullet took off the one tied around my waist. But those medicines protected me. Neither bullet hurt me. Hard as it is to believe, the medicine that had been tied around my waist came home, all the way back to Pryor, Montana, without me. The woman who made it said that it just appeared one day. These things happen. Non-Indians can't understand them, but they happen.

Another comfort to me was the ceremony in which one of my uncles prayed for my safe return. The ceremony was the Sun Dance. Because I was going overseas, my uncle danced for me, and after the ceremony, I went to him to give him cigarettes and all the other things that you give to a sun dancer. As I walked up, he said, "I saw you on crutches standing in the sunlight at the entrance to Sun Dance lodge." I knew then that I was going to be hurt in Vietnam, but that I would make it back. The next time my uncle saw me, I was on crutches because I had been shot through the leg. Those three things, the two medicines and the Sun Dance, they protected me. They brought me back.

Carson Walks Over Ice mimes a Vietnam exploit at the Crow Fair. Women in war bonnets portray Viet Cong. Walks Over Ice's war shirt was made by his mother according to a dream he received in Vietnam.

Carson Walks Over Ice (far left), who frequently participates in honor guard ceremonies on the Crow Reservation, was recognized on his return from Vietnam in the ceremony held for wounded veterans.

Chapter 7 FIGHTING THE CURVE

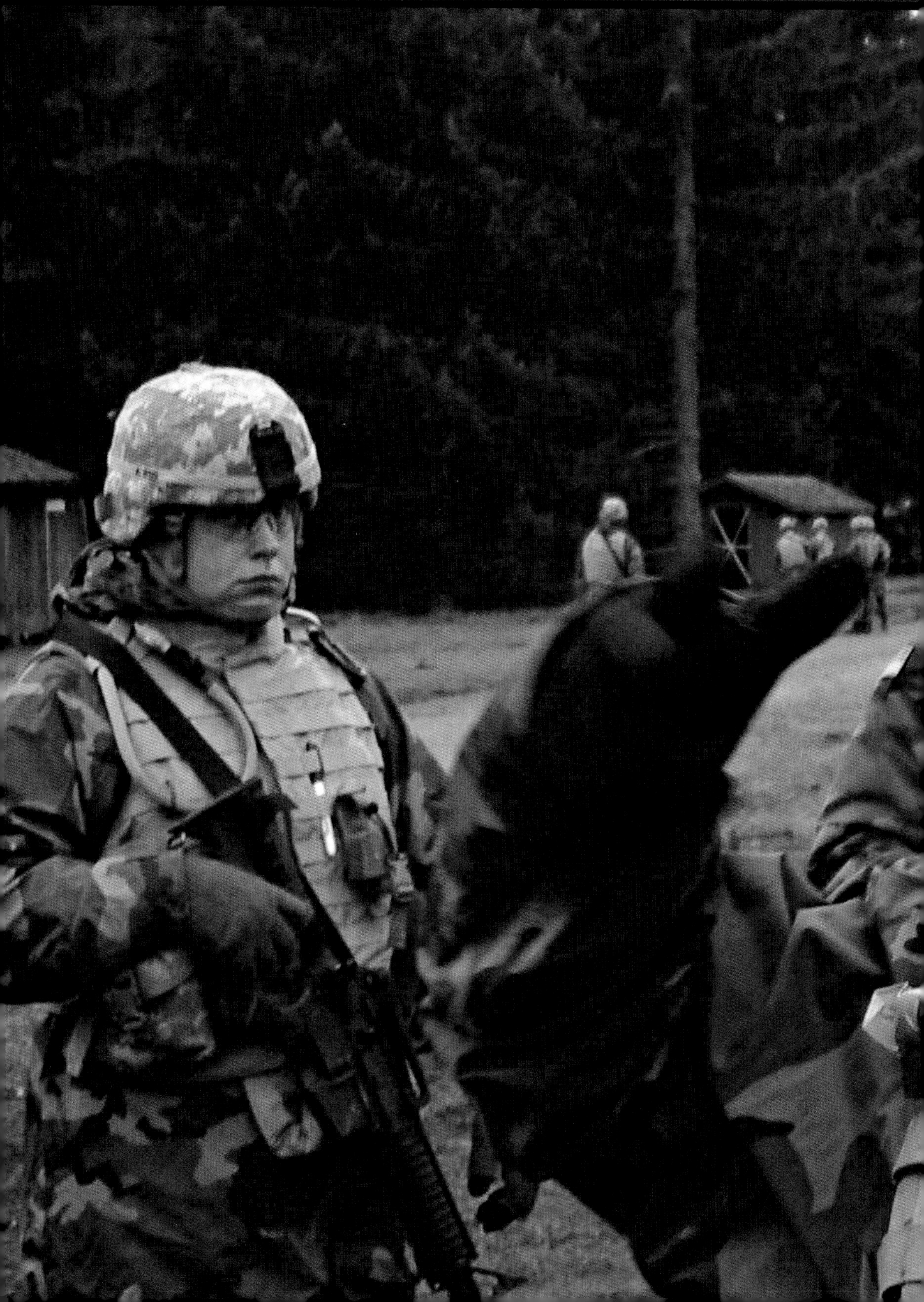

CPL. NATHAN GOOD IRON, OR YOUNG EAGLE, A MEMBER OF THE THREE AFFILIATED TRIBES, WAS KILLED BY A ROCKET-PROPELLED GRENADE IN AFGHANISTAN IN 2006.

THE SETTING SUN IN
FALLUJAH, IRAQ, CASTS
A GLOW ON A HAWK
FEATHER, A SACRED
OBJECT OWNED BY
COMBAT PHOTOGRAPHER
CHUCK BOERS.

In Afghanistan and Iraq American Indian men and women continue to serve in the armed forces in record numbers. A December 2005 tally by the Defense Department put the number of Native American/Alaskan Natives serving in the armed forces at almost 20,000. These conflicts, however, are unlike any other in America's military history. The enemy is zealous, elusive, and seldom in uniform. More often than not, the enemy arsenal consists of suicide bombers, booby traps, and hidden explosives. It is a type of warfare where "counting coup" is virtually impossible against a faceless enemy who mingles freely within a civilian population.

Another significant difference is the ability to communicate directly with soldiers in the war zones, thanks to the Internet. A number of Native soldiers are willing—even eager—to share their thoughts about following in a warrior tradition that is ages old, even though most are far removed from their traditional culture.

One of them is Army Specialist Benji Swanson, an Ojibwe from Leech Lake, Minnesota: "Where I grew up is now over run with drugs," he writes from Iraq. "I joined the military to get away for that and not expose my kids to it. I practiced the culture for a while and then it kind of faded away. I don't dance or drum, but I do see myself as a warrior—not just for other Indians but for myself."

His sentiments are echoed by Marine Sgt. James Dunham, an Apache:

I entered the Marine Corps in December of 1995 out of pride for my name sake and uncle, James F Bishop, who served the Corps during WWII as a communications wireman. I also have a firm belief that we as citizens owe a blood debt to our nation and to our ancestors. I was a teenager before I learned that First Nation Blood ran through my veins from my mother, who was part Apache. Only when I pressed family members did I start to learn the truth. As a child, I would walk into the wild by my self and find deer, porcupine, falcons and just sit and watch them for hours on end and never understand why. When the hunting season would start, my father would take me with him, although I did not hunt. He would call me his good luck because I could find game animals faster than he could. He never could figure it out why I was good at it. Honestly, I don't know either.

Although raised Christian and I have attended only one powwow—when I was five years old—I consider my self a Warrior. Yes, I do. After 9/11, I did not wait to be called up. I wanted to be on the war path like

"I GET RESTLESS IF I AM HOME TOO LONG, KNOWING THAT THERE IS STILL THE FIRE WITHIN ME TO FIGHT."

everyone else did, so I sent a letter to the Sergeant Major of the Marine Corps. Five days later I received a letter from his office, and two days later, I was on orders and on an Installation Reaction Force. Now I get restless if I am home too long, knowing that there is still the fire within me to fight and my brother Marines are still fighting. Because of that and my wife's support, I have deployed to Iraq in 2003, 2005, and now in 2007. Now I know what my Uncle James felt, and why he fought my grandmother so hard for permission to join the Marines when he was only 17 years old.

Sgt. Barry Crawford, a Cherokee in the Army National Guard from Oklahoma who has served three tours in Iraq, says:

I do practice some of the prayers, and some of [the] traditions. I carried a medicine bundle with me on my second tour. It was made for me a long time ago by a Cherokee medicine woman from the Webbers Falls area of Oklahoma. It was tied at the top in the traditional way with a leather thong. When I left Kuwait to return home, a customs agent made me open it. This, of course, is very much against my beliefs. I was really upset, so I chose not to bring a medicine bundle with me on this deployment for that very reason. I already regret that decision.

As of February 2007, approximately 40 Native Americans had been killed in Afghanistan and Iraq. One was Pvt. 1st Class Lori Piestewa, who died in Iraq in 2003. Half Hopi and half Hispanic, Piestewa has received national recognition as the first American Indian woman killed in combat. The 23-year-old soldier from Tuba City, Ariz., a mother of two, died from injuries when her unit, the 507th Maintenance Company, was ambushed near Nasiriyah.

Besides being the first Indian woman to die in combat, Piestewa now has another claim to fame: "Squaw Peak," formerly the name of the offensive and controversial mountain summit near Phoenix, is now "Piestewa Peak" in her honor.

Another was Nathan Good Iron, a corporal in the First Battalion of the North Dakota National Guard's 188th Air Defense Artillery. He died in Afghanistan on Thanksgiving Day 2006 when a rocket-propelled grenade struck his vehicle while on patrol. Good Iron, whose Indian name was Young Eagle, was the first member of the Three Affiliated Tribes on the Fort Berthold Reservation, to die in Afghanistan and Iraq. "Young Eagle," one of his eulogists declared, "your soul now flies on the wind with your brother eagles, keeping watch on those you left behind."

Ironically, even though much of the weaponry in use in the Middle East is on the cutting edge of technology, reflecting the computer-driven world of the 21st century, the Pentagon again has called upon American Indians to apply skills honed in another era to solve a modern military problem. Instead of code talkers, the U.S. Army now needs trackers who can find an enemy that eludes radar, motion detectors, cameras, and laser technology.

Alarmed at the ease with which Taliban and al Qaeda fighters were slipping in and out of Afghanistan and Iraq, the Pentagon in early 2007 sent an elite group of well-trained Native American marksmen and trackers to teach their skills to police units in Tajikistan and Uzbekistan, which border Afghanistan.

Known as the Shadow Wolves, the special unit was recruited from several tribes, including the Apache, Blackfeet, Cheyenne, Lakota, Navajo, and Tohono O'odham. Highly skilled in an ancient art and reminiscent of the Apache scouts who helped the U.S. Cavalry capture Geronimo a century

earlier, the Shadow Wolves are expert at noticing clues like twigs snapped by a passing person and pieces of fabric or strands of hair snagged on a branch. The professional trackers can tell how long a sliver of food has lain in the dirt or if someone has tried to conceal his tracks by strapping pieces of carpet to his shoes.

The Shadow Wolves were actually formed in the 1970s to help Drug Enforcement Agency officials track smugglers across hundreds of square miles of the Tohono O'odham tribal reservation, southwest of Tucson, Arizona. The Shadow Wolves use the skills they often learned as children tracking game animals on the reservation or finding free-ranging livestock that may have wandered away. "Instead of tracking an

The Shadow Wolves, traditionally trackers of drug smugglers, have taught police units in countries bordering Afghanistan how to track members of al Qaeda.

WARRIORS IN UNIFORM

AN ALL-CHEROKEE DRUM GROUP PARTICIPATES IN THE POWWOW HELD IN IRAQ IN 2004.

CHAPTER 7

animal, we now track human beings," says Bryan Nez, one of the Shadow Wolves. To qualify for the special unit, recruits must be one-quarter Indian.

Although Indians today are at the heart of the modern Army, old stereotypes are hard to erase. Sgt. Eli Painted Crow, a Yaqui soldier from Arizona who served in Iraq in 2004, in an interview on *Democracy Now!* recalled a military briefing that warned of the dangers out in "Indian country." "They called enemy territory 'Indian country,'" she said in disbelief. "I'm standing there, just listening to this briefing, and I'm just in shock that after all this time, after so many Natives have served and are serving and are dying [in the military in Iraq], that we are still the enemy, even if we're wearing the same uniform."

That same year some of those Native American soldiers managed to bring a little piece of real "Indian country" to Iraq by celebrating what must have been the first traditional powwow ever held in that part of the world. The goal was to promote cultural understanding of their heritage with fellow soldiers, sailors, and Marines, while bringing a piece of home to many of the Native Americans serving in Iraq.

The powwow was organized and hosted at the Al Taqaddum Air Base near Fallujah by the 120th Engineer Combat Battalion, a National Guard unit based in Okmulgee, Oklahoma. According to Army

Tomahawks fashioned from scrap or truck door metal are thrown in competition at a powwow in Iraq in 2004.

Capt. Shareen S. Fischer, the battalion chaplain and a Shinnecock Indian from New York, nearly 20 percent of the unit's soldiers boast some Indian blood. The two-day event featured dancing and singing, games such as stickball and tomahawk throwing, and traditional foods including genuine fry bread. The powwow ended, however, not with a traditional Native American ceremony, but a military one: the retirement of the colors.

The idea came from Sgt. Debra Mooney, a Choctaw from Idabel, Oklahoma. "We're brought up with [powwows]," she explained in an article about the event. "The beat of the drum is a part of the heartbeat of a Native American," said Mooney, who realized that the unit's year-long deployment to Iraq meant that many of the Indian soldiers would miss out on their family powwows back home. "I thought it was crazy at first," said Fischer in the article, but she took the idea to the battalion commander, who approved it even though it meant holding the powwow in a combat zone.

From start to finish, however, the planners had only a five-week window. To meet the deadline, Fischer and Mooney appointed soldiers to subcommittees to speed up the process. Dances and events had to be organized and rehearsed. Some Native dress, jewelry, and other essential regalia came from families back home. Others were fashioned from scraps of

"I THOUGHT TO MYSELF I MUST BE NUTS TRYING TO GO TO A POWWOW IN A COMBAT ZONE."

cloth, trash, and scavenged military gear. The drum came from a discarded 55-gallon oil can cut in half and canvas taken from a cot. Metal salvaged from truck doors formed the tomahawks used in a throwing contest. The stickball game featured sticks made from broom handles, with the baskets made from standard issue 5-50 parachute cord. An all-Cherokee group named Desert Thunder sang. The master of ceremonies was Staff Sgt. David Little, a Seminole. Head dancer for the powwow was 19-year-old Specialist George D. Macdonald, a Chickasaw from Sasakwa, Oklahoma. "I was brought up in a home where the native culture, the native spirit is very, very alive," he said in the article, "so being away from it for a long time brings you down when you think about the powwows back home."

Like MacDonald, all the Indian soldiers felt proud that they had participated in this historical event. Sgt. Barry Crawford, a Cherokee in the Army National Guard from Oklahoma, was present for only an hour or so at the end: "Mission dictated that I had other things to do at the time. But I was very impressed with the efforts of my brothers and sisters to arrange it all. The 120th Engineers is my home unit, and Sgt. Mooney is a friend of mine. I know they put a lot of effort into it, and I was very touched by it."

One of the eager participants was Master Sgt. Chuck Boers, an Army combat photographer and a Lipan Apache. His presence at the powwow was purely serendipitous. Recently returned from a combat mission in Samarra and the happy recipient of a four-day pass to Qatar, he met Betty Davis, a Cherokee soldier, as he was heading to his bunk. She asked him if he was going to the powwow at Al Taqaddum Air Base. "I thought she was pulling my leg," Boers says, but then she showed him the powwow flyer and said she was going. Since the dates for the powwow fell during his four-day leave, Boers obtained permission to change locations for his R & R and immediately jumped on a convoy going to Al Taqaddum.

En route to Al Taqaddum insurgents attacked the convoy, hitting the vehicles with small-arms fire and rocket-propelled grenades. "I thought to myself I must be nuts trying to go to a powwow in a combat zone," Boers, says, "but then outta nowhere a song popped into my head. It was ["NDN Kars"] by Keith Secola. I don't know why, but after that I knew everything was going to be okay and I was going to have a great four days."

Upon arriving at Al Taqaddum, he met Sergeant Mooney, who welcomed him and introduced him around. "It was a very surrealistic site. Here we were in the middle of a combat zone and bunch of Natives had gotten together to play stickball. Can you imagine that?" Since, to his knowledge, nothing like that had ever before been done in a combat zone, and since he is a combat photographer, Boers volunteered to document the event. "[Debra] had dedicated the powwow to all past and present veterans—so that was the theme for the powwow. It was a way to honor our fellow

"THE POWWOW WAS A…SUCCESS. I WAS AMAZED AT HOW MANY OTHER NATIVES MADE THE TRIP."

◆━━━◂●▸━━━◆

warriors. We all knew this was going to be a very special event and it would be like no other Powwow that any of us had ever attended."

Indeed it was—just like "Indian Fair Days [an annual powwow] back home," Boers marvels. "We played stickball, Indian marbles, and had a tomahawk throwing and blow gun contest the first day. That night we all got together for a little bit of singing, drumming and dancing. It wasn't a 49er [a dance party held following a powwow] or anything like that, but it was fun just hanging together."

During the powwow the next day there was an honoring ceremony for a fallen warrior, Specialist Raymond Bryan Estes III, a Ponca, of Charlie Battery, Fourth Battalion, First Field Artillery. His family had sent over a shawl to be used during the powwow. Debra Mooney placed the shawl over Specialist Leslie Montemayor, a soldier of Creek and Seminole heritage. After receiving the shawl, Leslie danced alone in the arena as everyone stood in honor and remembrance of their fallen brother warrior.

"The powwow was a great success," Boers says. "I was amazed at how many other Natives made the trip from all over Iraq. Most everyone had heard about the powwow by word of mouth, from a flyer, or in an email. It was just like back home."

During his 20 years as a combat photographer Boers has been deployed to all of the U.S. Army's hot spots—Grenada, Haiti, Bosnia, Kosovo, and the Middle East, including three tours in Iraq, during which he has received a Bronze Star, two Army Commendation Medals, two Purple Hearts, and a Polish service medal for his work as an adviser. "Everywhere I went," Boers says,

> I had always run into other Natives and we would usually all hang out together and tell stories about powwows, 49ers and other stuff like that, but nothing could have prepared me for my fourth tour to the Middle East during Operation Iraqi Freedom. Every Forward Operating Base (FOB) or mission I went on, I would run into another Native, it was something I had never experienced in my whole military career.

One of those warriors in uniform Boers met in Iraq was Sam Stitt, a Choctaw from Oklahoma serving in the Air Force. Stitt is a military linguist fluent in Arabic, with training in Iraqi dialects. At the time he was assigned to a small team operating in south central Iraq, on a base outside of An Najaf and was there for the siege of An Najaf in April 2004 as well as various other actions and firefights. Stitt says,

> Some of my duties would be considered classified, but I can say that we had numerous objectives and we were "outside the wire" every day. It was quite intense and actually not very fun at all. I was scared to death half the time really. I met Chuck, when he came down to An-Najaf for an anticipated "action."…We met up with

A ceremonial shawl was sent by the family of fallen warrior Raymond Bryan Estes to honor him at the 2004 powwow.

his team and helped them get settled in. Since I was the intelligence operator, I briefed him on the general security situation in our region.

Only after working together for several days did Boers and Stitt discover their shared Native heritage. Stitt says:

You don't usually make it a habit to randomly ask people what their ethnicity is. It was really kind of funny how it happened. Chuck said he needed to check his e-mail so I got him hooked up with a laptop in our office that had an internet connection. He told me he was checking out "Pow Wow Highway," which is a Native website. As he said it, I looked more closely at him and noticed his Native features. I was so excited I shouted, "Hey, I'm an enrolled Choctaw from Oklahoma," and I grabbed a photo of my kids in powwow regalia that I had on my desk. He then showed me some of his photos. Let me tell you, it was quite an experience to

SPC. BEN SWANSON
OF THE 1-565TH
QUARTERMASTER
COMPANY ATOP
HIS HUMVEE
EN ROUTE TO
CAMP ECHO IN IRAQ

run into another Native in the middle of a combat zone. He was down there for a couple of weeks and we would chat for hours about dancing, singing, family, and tribal issues. We talked about hitting the Pow Wow Highway together when we got home. In such a short amount of time it felt like we had been friends for years.

On the day of the mission, Boers and Stitt decided to create a wall mural (opposite) showing their tribal affiliations and marking the date and place, as a memento. They used bits of old plaster or rock from rubble to draw it, and a combat cameraman took their picture posing in front of it. "That photo somehow got back stateside," says Stitt, "and made its way onto the cover of *Indian Country Today*, May 9, 2004. We were featured on the same page as the Navajo code talkers. What an honor! The photo also made it into my tribal paper, *The Bishinik*."

Like his newfound friend, Stitt entered military service because, as a Native, it seemed the thing to do, although he is quick to admit that the idea of the Plains Indian in full buckskin regalia with feathers flying—the warrior image that is seared into the mainstream American consciousness—does not quite fit the Choctaw experience. "Most Choctaws are Christian or hold some hybrid Native-Christian belief," Stitt says:

We don't have the religious ceremonies for warriors one might find among the other so-called "warlike" tribes. However, we have a long history of military service. The first code talkers, in fact, were Choctaws during WWI. According to what I've heard it happened because a group of Okie Choctaws were chatting one day and an enterprising officer overheard them and came up with the scheme to have them send radio messages "in the clear" between Choctaw soldiers stationed at various positions on the battlefield.

Most Choctaw families have some tie to a veteran, Stitt says:

It's a tradition of sorts, and when I was young I just assumed that one day I would join. The young kids at the gatherings or powwows look up to the vets and it is something honorable—even if the war itself isn't. That is one reason non-Native vets show up at Native events. They know that they will get the respect they deserve, especially the Vietnam vets. Many of them had it rough fitting back into a society that could be hostile to them at times.

Like generations of warriors before him, Boers carries a medicine bundle and prepares himself spiritually before possible combat situations. These spiritual protectors he shares with Natives and non-Natives alike. For example, a month after their assignment in An Najaf, Stitt visited Camp Victory, Boers's home base near Baghdad. "We had about thirty minutes or so before Sam had to roll back out to An Najaf," Boers

SERGEANTS SAM STITT AND CHUCK BOERS, WHO DISCOVERED A SHARED NATIVE HERITAGE, POSE NEXT TO THEIR ARTWORK IN AN NAJAF, IRAQ.

CHAPTER 7

TRIBAL FLAGS

The first documented use of flags by North American Indians was during the Civil War.

According to Donald T. Healy, co-author of *Native American Flags,* the soldiers from the Five Civilized Tribes who fought for the Confederacy flew their own battle banner. The flag of the Choctaw Nation still features elements of that Civil War alliance.

The Arapaho of the Wind River Reservation in Wyoming designed one of the first of the modern-era tribal flags that are in widespread use today. The flag, which was adopted in 1956, grew out of the need for an appropriate way to honor tribal veterans.

Besides promoting tribal identity, the flags are also a statement of tribal sovereignty. As Healy points out, a series of landmark federal decisions in the last quarter of the 20th century that buttressed the right of Native self-government inspired many of the tribes to design and fly their own flags. The proliferation of tribal casinos was also a factor.

Master Sgt. Chuck Boers (left) and Staff Sgt. James Dunham hold up the Lipan Apache Tribal Flag at Multi-National Division Central-South, Camp Echo, Ad Diwaniyah, Iraq.

"AFTER I FINISHED BLESSING MY WAR PONY, THE SOLDIERS ASKED IF I WOULD BLESS THEM."

says, "but that was more than enough time for us to catch up on what we had both been doing."

Before Stitt left, Boers gave him some sage and cedar and two hawk feathers for his children. That evening, at the nightly update briefing, it was announced that a convoy going from Baghdad to An Najaf had been attacked. "My first thoughts," Boers says,

> were about Sam. That night I prayed to the Creator to look out for him. The next day when I checked my email, there was one from Sam telling me about the firefight and the attack on his convoy. It was a close one for him and the others that day. I know when Sam passes those Hawk feathers to his children it will have a very special meaning for them.

A month later, Boers was back in the fight. This time he was sent to Fallujah to photograph operations with Apache Troop, Second Battalion, Seventh Regiment, First Cavalry Division. As the three soldiers assigned to help him watched, Boers hung a hawk feather, did a small blessing with some cedar and sage, and painted the side of his "War Pony"—an armored all-terrain vehicle, which has replaced the jeep in the modern Army. He says:

> I thought my soldiers would think me crazy or something as I did my Native spiritual preparations, but I didn't care. Then, to my surprise, after I finished blessing my War Pony, the soldiers asked if I would bless them. I am glad

I did because it was kinda rough for us in Fallujah. The squad we were with got hit real hard and one soldier, SPC Jose A. Velez, was killed.…For his actions that day Velez was awarded the Silver Star along with two other members of his squad. Now when I gourd dance, I remember not only our past, present and future warriors, but I also always remember and honor SPC Velez and the other Soldiers I served with that day in Fallujah.

True to their promise in Iraq, Boers and Stitt did link up stateside and attend a few powwows together. "It was great—almost like the 'band of brothers' cliché," Stitt says. He adds:

> But it's not a cliché. We exchanged gifts. He presented me with hawk feathers and an Eagle spike and I gave him a beaded knife sheath. Once he let me borrow a uniform and his Native Color Guard allowed me to participate in the posting of colors. Since that time I've been dancing at powwows in the Northwest and often I am asked to be a flag bearer. Several times I've been given an honor song and danced solo, with the crowd standing. It is such a great feeling.

And like Boers, Stitt also remembers fallen warriors as he dances, like fellow Choctaw Lance Cpl. Hatak Yearby, who died in a vehicle explosion in Al Anbar Province in May 2006. As Stitt says modestly, "It's how Indians honor their warriors."

WARRIORS IN UNIFORM

THE ALL-CHEROKEE DRUM GROUP TAKES A BREAK DURING THE 2004 POW-WOW IN IRAQ.

Chuck Boers's Story

Master Sgt. Chuck Boers is typical of many of today's Indian soldiers. His mother is Chiricahua/Lipan Apache and Western Band Cherokee from Oklahoma. His father is a Dutchman who came to America from Holland after World War II with his family. His parents divorced soon after he was born. While growing up, Boers learned about his Apache culture from his grandfather and his Cherokee culture from his grandmother. Although his mother's family was from Oklahoma and Texas, he grew up primarily in California. "One might think being so far away from our tribal roots that we would lose touch of who we are, but that was not the case. My grandparents showed and shared with me and my sisters the richness and vibrancy of our culture."

Nonetheless, it was not always easy growing up as an urban Indian, never really quite fitting in the red or white worlds. It was Boers's family and other Indian friends who helped him accept life in both worlds. He credits Betty Coulter, a Cherokee, and other Title IV (Indian Education Act) Native counselors with helping him get through his teenage years.

What stand out were the powwows, the tribal

Sgt. Johan "Chuck" Boers with his mother, Virginia, and brother Craig before leaving for Korea in 1985

ceremonies, and Title IV events that he attended. "My favorite part of the Powwow was Grand Entry when the Veterans would bring in the Colors and then afterwards they would do an honor dance," Boers says. "I was taught that we always welcome home our warriors with songs and dances, and my thoughts always turned towards my parents, uncles, and other relatives who had served in the military. I was proud of them and of the sacrifices that they had made for all of us."

The day Boers graduated from high school and got his diploma he was on top of the world, he says. What made the day more special and memorable, however, was the fact that his Title IV counselor Betty Coulter gave him his first eagle feather, telling him she was proud of the young man he had become and that the feather would keep him safe while he was in the Army. "I have carried that eagle feather with me all over the world—on deployments, on peacekeeping missions, into combat, and one day after I retire," he says, "I will pass that eagle feather on to the next young warrior."

Boers joined the Army in August 1982, just before the start of his senior year of high school. His recruiter was his mother, Virginia, a sergeant first class who spent 11 of her 20 years in the Army as a recruiter. "The joke in the family was that my Mother was low on her recruiting numbers that month and needed to put me in the Army in order to make her numbers...," Boers says, adding:

> In truth, I have always looked up to my parents and my other relatives who had served in the military. In fact, our family has served in every war that the United States has had since World War I. We even had family serve as Army scouts in the late 1800s. I wouldn't call us patriotic, but we are proud to serve our people and protect our way of life. I knew I wanted to be part of that world. It is part of our culture to be warriors.

Boers's mother did not see herself as a warrior, but she did see the Army as a unique opportunity for a woman. "It opened a lot of doors for me," she says. "Back then there weren't a whole lot of jobs for a woman that paid as good as the military and taught you a skill at the same time. While in the WACs I was in transportation and administration, but my last eleven years I was an Army recruiter. I was proud and pleased that Chuck was continuing our family and tribal tradition—to serve in the military."

Virginia, the oldest of five children, had four brothers, and all of them followed her into the Army. Three were combat medics and one served in the Air Defense Artillery. One served two tours in Vietnam as a Special Forces medic, followed by a tour in Desert Storm. As if a 20-year military career was not challenge enough, she also had six children of her own and raised another one as well.

Boers thanks his mother not only for getting him into the Army but also for helping him make it through boot camp. As luck

Sgt. Chuck Boers has more than 20 years of service in the military and says, "It is part of our culture to be warriors."

would have it, he was assigned to the same camp and same unit his mother had been assigned to when she went through basic training —Fort McCullen, Alabama, Third Platoon, Delta Company, Second Battalion. "When the training got tough, I would tell myself—'If my Mom, who is less than 5 feet tall, did this, so can I.' It was like she was there pushing me all through basic training. I used to wonder about the odds of going through basic training in the same unit as my mother and living in the same barracks she had lived in so many years ago. My mother...felt that it would give us a different kind of bond, not only as mother and son, but also as soldiers. My grandmother had always told me the Creator had a plan and reason for everything that happens. We may not understand it at the time, but eventually it might be revealed to us. That's the only way I could explain it."

OPENING CEREMONY AT A POWWOW ON THE ROSEBUD SIOUX RESERVATION, SOUTH DAKOTA. THE VETERANS HOLD COUP STICKS AND TRIBAL AS WELL AS AMERICAN FLAGS.

MASTER SGT. CHUCK BOERS CARRIES IN THE EAGLE STAFF DURING A POWWOW IN SHENANDOAH, VIRGINIA, WHILE HE WAS HOME FROM IRAQ ON R&R.

Native American veterans are honored by their family and their tribe, both before going into service and upon their return. The most visible expression of the honor Indian veterans receive is at powwows.

For Native Americans, powwows can be everything from a family reunion to a religious ceremony. Largely associated with Plains tribes, powwows were primarily spiritual gatherings to celebrate certain tribal events or individuals through songs and dancing.

When Indians were moved onto reservations at the end of the 19th century, the meaning of their dancing changed. They began to use dance—the Ghost Dance is a prime example—as a way to ask for spiritual help and guidance to cope with changes being forced on them by the U.S. government. The government, in turn, regarded the dancing as inflammatory, a hopeless attempt to hold on to a lost way of life, and banned them. The ban was eventually lifted in 1933, and dancing resumed its important position in tribal culture. Indeed, powwows today are a vital part of keeping tribal traditions alive.

At many powwows, Indian veterans are honored. They can be asked to lead the Grand Entry, to carry the tribal and U.S. flags, and to dance. In recent years, powwows dedicated to Indian veterans have appeared across the country. One of these, held annually in November, is the National Native American Veterans Pow Wow. Marine Corps Gunnery Sgt. Shawn Arnold, one of the event co-founders, told the American Forces Press Service, "We hold the powwow to pay tribute to Native Americans who put their lives at risk to ensure the survival of future generations."

One of the veterans frequently honored at powwows was Lt. Billy Walkabout, a Cherokee who is often cited as the most decorated Native American soldier of the Vietnam War. A member of Company F, 58th Infantry Regiment, 101st Airborne Division, Walkabout received the Distinguished Service Cross, the nation's second highest military award; five Bronze Stars; five Silver Stars; and six Purple Hearts, as well as the Legion of Valor and five Army Commendation Medals. A few of his heroic actions—in which he saved several of his fellow soldiers—are recounted in *Eyes of the Eagle,* by Gary A. Linderer, one of the wounded men he saved. Linderer called Walkabout "a hero earning a Medal of Honor before my eyes."

Walkabout, who died in 2007 at the age of 57, had a troubled life after Vietnam. He had medical problems related to his exposure to the defoliant Agent Orange, and he endured painful memories. "War is not hell," he told an interviewer in 1986. "It's worse." He struggled with depression and thoughts of suicide, spending months in self-isolation. His only solace, according to his family, was at powwows.

THE ELDERS VOWED, "YOUR SPIRIT AND OURS WILL PROTECT YOU."

Less visible but nonetheless important to Indian military personnel are private rituals and religious ceremonies, such as the blessing Vietnam veteran Duane Simpson received before he left his home on the Colville Indian Reservation to join the Army in 1964. Simpson's experiences were featured in one of a series of articles the Spokane, Washington, *Spokesman Review* ran on Thomas Watt, a Colville Indian who served in Vietnam.

Tribal elders took the 17-year-old boy into the mountains to purify him and prepare him spiritually. According to *Spokesman Review* writer Kevin Graman, Simpson's uncle had to break ice in a stream for the sweat house ceremony, which included being cleansed with cedar smoke and plunging four times into the frigid water.

At the conclusion of the ceremony, the elders vowed, "Your spirit and ours will protect you." At a 2005 veterans reunion, wrote Graman, Simpson theorized that the protection he received was "as good a reason as any" for his surviving two tours of duty.

For the tribes with a warrior tradition, their military societies help keep that tradition alive. One of the most celebrated is the Ton-Kon-Ga, or Black Legs Society, of the Kiowa Indian Nation of Oklahoma (see pages 182-183).

How the society got its name is unknown. Some think it derives from the trail dust that blackened the legs of warriors after a long trek. Others suggest it is in honor of Kiowa warriors who survived an attempt by enemies to defeat them by setting fire to the prairie grasses during a battle.

The society flourished during the 19th century until driven underground around 1890 by the Bureau of Indian Affairs, which sought to eradicate all forms of traditional religion practiced by America's Native peoples. By 1928, the society had ceased to function until its revitalization by Kiowa military veterans 30 years later. One of the veterans was Gus Palmer, who dedicated the revival to the memory of his brother Lyndreth, killed in World War II. Thanks to the efforts of the few surviving society members, who taught the songs, dances, and traditions to younger military veterans, the Black Leggings Society, as it is now known, is active and vibrant.

Membership traditionally has been restricted to enrolled Kiowa (or certified tribal members), although reportedly some Comanche have become members. Members wear black leggings (or paint their legs black) and a red cape, which symbolizes the red cape captured from a Mexican army officer. The society emblem is a staff wrapped in otter fur. The society tepee features the battle designs of a famous 19th-century war chief on one side and the service crests of today's Kiowa servicemen on the other. It also features the names of the nine Kiowa servicemen killed in combat since World War I.

The society holds mourning feasts, conducts cedaring ceremonies, and performs graveside tributes for deceased members. At each biannual ceremony the society provides a meal to all in attendance. Female relatives of society members perform scalp and victory dances using men's lances and

A Kiowa Black Leggings ceremony. The society, which had all but disappeared 100 years ago, has been revitalized by Kiowa military veterans in the past 50 years.

feathered headdresses to open the afternoon events, while inside the tepee the men prepare for the five types of dances they will perform. Once a year the society performs the *Tsat'hoigya,* or Reverse Dance, during which a combat veteran stops the drum and recites a personal battle exploit.

The society's most distinguished member was 1st Sgt. Pascal Poolaw. A veteran of three wars—World War II, Korea, and Vietnam—Sergeant Poolaw is acclaimed as America's most decorated "warrior in uniform." He earned 42 medals, badges, citations, and campaign ribbons for combat service and for valor, including three Silver Stars, five Bronze Stars, three Purple Hearts (one in each war), three Army Commendation Medals, and the Distinguished Service Cross. He was also nominated for the Medal of Honor.

Although Sergeant Poolaw had retired in 1962, he reentered the Army five years later in an effort to keep his son Lindy from having to go to Vietnam. Another son, Pascal Poolaw, Jr., had already served in Vietnam, losing a leg in an explosion, and Army regulations prohibited two members of the same family from serving in a combat zone without their consent. But he was too late. Upon reaching the point of departure on the West Coast, Sergeant Poolaw discovered that Lindy had left for Vietnam the day before, so he decided to follow him.

WARRIORS IN UNIFORM

A SCENE FROM THE CLEANSING AND NAMING CEREMONY FOR DESERT STORM VETERAN RON BIG BACK ON THE NORTHERN CHEYENNE RESERVATION NEAR LAME DEER, MONTANA

CHAPTER 8

"THE SIOUX GOT THE GLORY, THE CROWS GOT THE LAND, BUT THE CHEYENNE DID THE FIGHTING."

Having father and son in combat at the same time was nothing new to the Poolaw family. Pascal had served in World War II with his father and two brothers. But this time luck ran out for him. Four months after arriving in Vietnam he was killed in action while trying to carry a wounded soldier to safety. Poolaw had four sons. Each entered the Army, and three served in Vietnam.

Another Plains Indian tribe that has revitalized its warrior traditions is the Northern Cheyenne Nation of Montana. The Cheyenne were one of the premier warrior peoples of the northern Plains. Indeed, there is a popular saying in Indian country about Custer's Last Stand that expresses well the role of the Cheyenne on the battlefields of the American West: "The Sioux got the glory, the Crows got the land, but the Cheyenne did the fighting." For its tenacious resistance to westward expansion the tribe paid a terrible price in blood and tears. It still feels the effects of the government's relentless efforts to curb the warrior spirit. Nonetheless, its young men and women have been well represented in the armed forces of the United States since the end of the Indian wars.

One of its modern-day warriors is Ron Big Back, a veteran of Desert Storm, the conflict that set the stage for the Iraq War a decade later. While in Kuwait, Army Private Big Back had had a frightening dream: He was riding a beautiful spotted horse and he was dressed as a traditional Cheyenne warrior. He and his horse came to a river and the horse splashed into it

without hesitation. The water got deeper and the horse began swimming, and as the horse struggled across it was beset by many poisonous snakes that bit it repeatedly. Although gravely hurt, the horse managed to reach the far bank, but it then collapsed and died. Big Back was able to step ashore unhurt, but he grieved for his fallen horse. What, he wondered, could the dream mean?

Worried, he wrote to his father, who showed the letter to Tom Rock Roads, a Vietnam veteran and a respected spiritual leader on the Northern Cheyenne Reservation. Rock Roads had a ready explanation: Ron Big Back was coping with evil spirits in Kuwait and would need a cleansing ceremony as soon as he returned. Rock Roads, a combat veteran himself, would perform the ceremony.

Meanwhile, another letter arrived from Kuwait, this one from Big Back's commanding officer telling the family that their son had performed heroically in the face of a Scud missile attack: Private Big Back had been on guard duty one night when a missile exploded near his position. At the time it was believed that Scud missiles spread harmful biological and chemical contaminants upon exploding. But ignoring the threat to his own safety, Private Big Back had alerted his sleeping comrades with a Cheyenne war cry and rushed to put out the ensuing fire.

When Big Back returned from Kuwait in May 1991, his family decided to conduct a ceremony confirming the revival and

Ron Big Back receives a coup stick at his
cleansing and naming ceremony. The stick is adorned with a simulated scalp lock.

continuation of centuries-old traditions in which war heroes received the praise and plaudits of friends and relatives. Some 100 people attended the ceremony including Austin Two Moons, whose grandfather fought Custer at the Little Bighorn, and Ben Nighthorse Campbell, then a congressman from Colorado.

Also present was the Northern Cheyenne Honor Guard, each representing branches of the U.S. armed forces, and a drum group. Arrayed in front of the emcee's lectern was a complete Iraqi soldier's uniform, including the boots, that Private Big Back had appropriated while serving in Kuwait.

Before the ceremony began, Big Back's father read the letter commending his son for bravery. The effort was almost too much for him and he began to cry. "Thank you so much for coming to witness this," he said. "I am so proud of my son. I am so proud to know that he is a Cheyenne warrior like his ancestors."

Private Big Back first underwent a purification ceremony with the incense of sage to cleanse him of any evil spirits that lingered around him after his combat experience. Tom Rock Roads performed the ceremony assisted by his friend Jimmy Red Cloud. Then Rock Roads gave Ron Big Back a new name, Charging Eagle. As part of the cleansing and naming ceremony, Rock Roads used a coup stick adorned with a simulated scalp lock, representing a scalp he had taken in Vietnam.

At the conclusion of the ceremony, Rock Roads presented Charging Eagle to his family and friends as the drummers and singers heralded him with a warrior's honor song. Then, taking charcoal from a large bonfire, Charging Eagle blessed and smudged the faces of each of the spectators, who helped themselves from the large pile of cloth, blankets, packaged goods, and other items the family had assembled for the giveaway in his honor.

The ceremony ended with a scalp dance led by Rock Roads and Charging Eagle accompanied by the Northern Cheyenne Honor Guard, who led the spectators around the bonfire and past the Iraqi uniform spread out on the ground in the dance area.

Each of the women picked up a stick from a nearby pile and used it to strike the uniform—"to count coup" on the symbolic Iraqi soldier—as they danced past. All the while, the honor guard fired off rounds

An honor ceremony for Black Legs Society member Pascal Poolaw in 1952. Poolaw would later be killed in Vietnam.

WARRIORS IN UNIFORM

SHE SAID IT WAS GOOD TO KNOW THAT SOME OF THE OLD-TIME CEREMONIES WERE COMING BACK.

◆━━━━◄ ● ►━━━━◆

of blank ammunition from their rifles and the women burst forth with spontaneous "trilling." A sudden thunder and lightning storm put out the fire and sent everyone rushing to their cars.

An elderly Cheyenne woman who was later asked if she had been present at the Big Back ceremony said no, but she had heard about it. She said it was good to know that some of the old-time ceremonies were coming back. The last time this ceremony had been performed, she believed, was after the Second World War. "I tell you," she laughed, "it was really something to see those old ladies dancing with those German and Japanese scalps!"

Adjoining the Northern Cheyenne Reservation is the Crow Reservation. Like their Cheyenne neighbors, the Crow also honor their veterans with celebrations and ceremonies. For example, when Crow soldiers returned to the reservation after World War II, their relatives would stage a welcome right at the train station and a week or two later hold a reception.

As World War II veteran Joseph Medicine Crow (see Chaper 4) recalled in *Counting Coup,* his welcome home reception in January 1946 was particularly memorable because he missed the gala at the Lodge Grass, Montana, train station.

En route his train stopped in Sheridan, Wyoming, for about a half hour, so he took the opportunity to buy a hamburger at a favored diner. "Louie could make a dime hamburger taste like a New York-cut sirloin," Medicine Crow recalls. "Boy, I sure missed those hamburgers while I was overseas."

Because of the detour, he missed the train and the large crowd waiting to welcome him. "My mother was ready with a stack of new Pendleton blankets to spread from the train to the singers, some 60 feet away," he remembers.

As Medicine Crow got off the train at Lodge Grass, he says, "I was supposed to walk along the row of blankets and start dancing as I reached the singers. Well, this didn't take place....Poor Mom, she sure must have been disappointed."

As a result, Medicine Crow had to wait for his reception, which was held that weekend at the Tribal Dance Hall in Lodge Grass. "As I walked into the hall," he recalls,

> people along the way shook my hands, relatives hugged me, and admiring girls kissed me....The drummers [then] sang the war honor song of my grandfather Chief Medicine Crow. I danced around the floor with my relatives dancing behind me.

Medicine Crow was then asked by some of the elders at the reception to tell everyone his combat experiences. He recalled being taken aback by the request, saying, "I had never thought about my activities on the battlefield as 'war deeds,' except when I captured the horses." He says:

> I told the elders about my hand-to-hand encounter with the German soldier and how I took his gun away from him. Then I related the time I

WARRIORS IN UNIFORM

WILLIAM UNDER BAG-
GAGE, WHOSE NEPHEW
CPL. BRETT LUNDSTROM
WAS KILLED IN IRAQ,
WALKS WITH A PHOTO-
GRAPH OF THE SOLDIER
DURING HIS WAKE.

CHAPTER 8

"THE WORDS IN MY HONOR SONG…REFLECT THE PRIDE WE CROW PEOPLE CHERISH…FOR OUR WARRIOR HEROES."

was in charge of the detail of soldiers that went after dynamite so the big guns along the Siegfried line could be blasted. And I told them about sneaking into the German camps and stealing the horses belonging to the SS officers. For those four coups, I was declared a full-fledged Crow war chief.

After the recitation of his war deeds, Medicine Crow's family started a giveaway, which is done to honor someone in Crow society. "I know in white society when someone is honored that person gets the presents," Medicine Crow says,

> but that is not the way it is done in Crow society. When someone succeeds, he or she gives presents to those who helped make that success possible, like…relatives, teachers, and friends. My mother gave away a stack of new Pendleton blankets, quilts, and other nice things.

Medicine Crow's father gave away a horse with a new saddle and bridle. The giveaway was followed by a feast.

At the welcome home reception, Medicine Crow was given the name High Bird, after a warrior from the Whistling Water clan, and given his right to be a camp crier, or announcer. He also had an honor song composed for him:

> *High Bird, you are a great soldier!*
> *High Bird, you fought the mighty Germans!*

> *High Bird, you counted coup on them!*
> *High Bird, you are a great soldier!*

Medicine Crow uses his honor song in tribal ceremonies. "When it is played, I dance and my relatives follow me. The words in my honor song, like the songs of the Crow chiefs before me, reflect the pride we Crow people cherish to this day for our warrior heroes."

When Private Medicine Crow returned home from Germany he arrived by train. Sixty years later, Crow veterans are met at the airport. Otherwise little has changed. Typical is the reception accorded U.S. Marine Cpl. Ivan Wilson, who returned home on leave after serving seven months as part of Operation Iraqi Freedom (see page 180).

Three months earlier, less than 500 miles away in the little Pine Ridge Reservation town of Kyle, South Dakota, there had been another honor ceremony for a Marine corporal, but this one was as sad as the other joyous.

The returning Marine was Brett Lundstrom, the first Oglala Sioux fatality of Operation Iraqi Freedom. A procession also marked his return. At first it consisted only of a hearse, two vans with 12 Marines in dress uniform, and a police escort, but as it wound its way to the middle of the reservation, it continued to grow as cars and pickup trucks parked along the road took their place at the end of the line.

The procession stopped where a dozen or so horsemen, several wearing eagle feather war bonnets, waited alongside the road with

Chris Lively, severely wounded while serving in Iraq,
is an enthusiastic moccasin maker for Project Moccasin, which carries on the traditional practice.

a small empty horse-drawn wagon. After lifting the flag-draped casket from the hearse and placing it gently on the bed of the old wagon, the Marines stood at attention. At the command of one of the riders, the procession set off. The saddle of the last horse was empty.

Upon reaching the Little Wound High School, the Marines carried the flag-draped casket into the gymnasium and placed it before a 30-foot-tall tepee at one end of the hardwood floor. Then, beginning a rotation that would last for two days and nights, two Marines positioned themselves at opposite ends of the opened casket.

Seated in the gymnasium were friends and relatives of Lundstrom's family as well as numerous Lakota veterans, who had come to

honor the fallen warrior. Most of the veterans were wearing their service caps and uniforms, many of them emblazoned with unit patches, ribbons, and medals. Tucked into some of the caps was a single eagle feather.

Like Ivan Wilson, his Crow comrade in arms, Brett Lundstrom boasted a distinguished warrior heritage. Ironically, his ancestors often earned their warrior status fighting the Crow, once the mortal enemies of the Lakota. One of his distant relatives was Iron Hail, also known as Dewey Beard, who fought against Goes Ahead and Custer in the Battle of the Little Bighorn. Another ancestor was the great Lakota leader Red Cloud. Now, though, the Crow and Lakota are on the same side. One of Lundstrom's uncles was killed at the

Battle of the Bulge during World War II. Another uncle died in Korea. His father, Ed Lundstrom, had recently retired from the Marines. Brett served three months in Afghanistan in 2004, before going to Iraq, where he was killed by small-arms fire in Fallujah. Corporal Lundstrom was 22.

The *Rocky Mountain News,* which covered the ceremony, reported that John Around Him, who emceed the ceremony for Brett Lundstrom, explained, "Brett earns the American flag from his government. From his people, he earns the eagle feather," a tribal badge of honor for military service.

That night Corporal Lundstrom, who had never lived on the reservation—because his father was stationed elsewhere during his military career—was given a new name by his great-uncle, Birgil Kills Straight. As the *Rocky Mountain News* reported, Kills Straight explained the name's significance: "Before he enters the spirit world, it's important for him to have an Indian name, because that's how the ancestors will know him."

The name Lundstrom received was Wanbli Isnala, or Lone Eagle, because, as Kills Straight explained, placing the eagle feather on Lundstrom's chest, "He, alone, above everything else, is an eagle. He will fly to the highest reaches of the universe. He may bring back news to us in our dreams."

Not all tribes glorify warfare even though they honor their soldiers. For some, especially

An eagle feather was placed on the body of Cpl. Brett Lundstrom during the naming ceremony that prepared him properly for his journey into the afterlife.

WARRIORS IN UNIFORM

"HOW CAN I BLEND THE WHITE MAN'S MILITARY PURPOSE WITH THE HOPI CULTURE?"

the Pueblo peoples of the Southwest, there is conflict between being a soldier and the possibility of taking another human's life.

This was well expressed in a 2003 interview in the *Arizona Republic* with Cliff Qotsaquahu, then commander of American Legion Hopi Post 80. "Hopis are very reserved in talking about their combat experiences," he said. "They think, 'How can I be a good Hopi, knowing I possibly killed somebody, or did kill somebody? How can I blend the White man's military purpose with the Hopi culture?'" Traditional ceremonies, he said, provide a measure of solace.

In the cleansing ceremony, Qotsaquahu explained, the veteran's paternal aunts escort him into the village, where they wash his hair and give him a new name. Cleansing ceremonies of up to four days are also performed by spiritual leaders. But, Qotsaquahu said, "there are no statues among the Hopi for those killed in combat. We don't memorialize them. We believe that they have joined the Cloud People Society and that someday we will join them."

Another cultural practice somewhat modified by the realities of Indian life in the 21st century is the making of moccasins. Traditionally, a warrior went into battle wearing new moccasins made for him by one of his loved ones—a grandmother, a mother, a sister, a wife. The new moccasins were to see the warrior home safely from battle or ease his transition into the spirit world.

This practice continues in Project Moccasin, although its volunteers often have no idea who will receive the fruits of their labors. Sponsored by the National Native American

Veterans Association of Oklahoma City and the American Indian Chamber of Commerce of Oklahoma, Project Moccasin was initiated by Anthony DeClue, a Lakota veteran living in St. Cloud, Minnesota, who is one of the moccasin makers. "I spent seven years in the Special Forces and I was disconnected from my heritage," DeClue explained to the *Native American Times*:

> I want the warriors in Afghanistan and Iraq to feel connected. When they take off their boots and put their feet in the moccasins they might feel a little closer to where they are from. What I do is thread them up. Another guy does the leatherwork—he stamps the leather with eagle feathers and sends it to me and I start painting them. The moccasins are smudged and we put a dream catcher and a piece of Mother Earth in each one so that our warriors will come home.

Another of the moccasin makers is Sgt. Chris Lively, an Army specialist who lives in Charlotte, Texas, with his wife and five children.

For Lively the project is especially meaningful because he is one of the Native soldiers who almost did not make it back from Iraq, suffering life-threatening injuries twice on the same day. He was riding in a vehicle that hit an improvised explosive device made of four 155 mortar rounds wired together with additional explosives. Fifteen minutes later, while chasing the insurgents who had exploded the first IED, his vehicle hit a

WARRIORS IN UNIFORM

VETERANS JOSEPH MEDI-
CINE CROW, ANDREW BIRD
IN GROUND, KENNETH OLD
COYOTE, AND HENRY OLD
COYOTE FORM THE HONOR
GUARD AT A CEREMONY ON
THE CROW RESERVATION.

CHAPTER 8

THE RETURN CEREMONY FOR MARINE CPL. IVAN WILSON

When 23-year-old Marine Cpl. Ivan Wilson came home to Billings, Montana, in 2006, he met a crowd of close to 100 relatives, tribal members, and a drum group wearing eagle feather headdresses and beaded vests. His father greeted him with a framed picture featuring photographs of his son's warrior ancestors.

Wilson stood at attention as a fellow tribal veteran placed a war bonnet on his head as part of a ceremony that featured praise songs and chants, warrior dances, and a procession around the terminal. Many of his Crow family members and friends carried small American flags and Pendleton blankets and wore T-shirts and shawls bearing his photograph and the Marine Corps insignia. Typical of the Crow women's welcome for returning warriors, the blankets and shawls had earlier been spread out on the lobby floor as Wilson made his descent of the stairway.

At the conclusion of the ceremony, reported the *Billings Gazette*, which covered the ceremony, Burton Pretty on Top, speaking for the family, told the fascinated throng of travelers and airport personnel: "What you have witnessed was a young man honored in the Crow traditional way."

Wilson, who served as a military police officer at Camp Fallujah in Iraq, has a distinguished warrior heritage. One of his relatives was Goes Ahead, a scout for the Seventh Cavalry at the Battle of the Little Bighorn. Another was Big Shoulderblade, a pipe carrier in Crow war parties led by Plenty Coups, the renowned war chief who spoke at the dedication of the Tomb of the Unknown Soldier at Arlington Ceremony. Ivan Wilson's grandfather, Raymond Bear Below, served with the U.S. Army in both World War II and Korea. Before his death in 1997, he often expressed the wish that his grandson would also join the military. Ivan was happy to honor that wish. "I've just always believed that Indians should be warriors," he told the *Billings Gazette*.

Cpl. Ivan Wilson was honored following his return from Iraq.

"WE MAY HAVE BEEN A CONQUERED PEOPLE, BUT WE WERE NOT A DEFEATED PEOPLE."

◆————◆———●———◆————◆

500-pound bomb that had failed to explode on impact and was recovered by the insurgents.

Sergeant Lively suffered a broken neck and other injuries that left him 100 percent disabled. Nonetheless, he is able to make moccasins and he is one of Project Moccasin's most enthusiastic supporters. In fact, he made one pair of moccasins for Sgt. Chuck Boers. Like so many of the Indians in the military, Lively sees himself as a soldier carrying on a warrior tradition. As part of a nine-man team—a modern-day "war party" —he helped capture three insurgents who had killed 14 Iraqi soldiers. "If you can count coup by taking away an enemy's weapon, then I did this," he says. During his entire time in Iraq, Lively carried a medicine bundle. His only regret was not having a bow and arrows with him. "I am very much into archery and I think if I had been able to take my bow and arrows to Iraq, it would have frightened the insurgents."

Lively grew up not knowing much about his Indian heritage. He was born in Washington, D.C., but his mother gave him up for adoption. He did not learn that he was part Iroquois, Apache, and Cherokee until almost grown. His mother was Iroquois and Cherokee, his father part Apache. Lively says:

Once I did know, I grasped my heritage with relish, learning as much as I could about who I am and who my people were. I took that with me to Iraq. The skills I learned came in useful in the desert badlands—the ability to pick out the bad guys in a crowd, the ability to see hidden explosive devices when hardly a track was made. Indians have a natural sense, almost like ESP. Maybe it is in our DNA. I don't want to exaggerate, but it is an unexplainable heightened sense of surroundings, an awareness, that spooks non-Indians. For example, during one of my missions in Iraq I had a terrible sense of foreboding, that something was wrong. I told the driver to stop. I was the gunner. Just as we stopped an I.E.D. exploded in front of us.

Besides serving in Iraq, Lively was with the Fifth Special Forces in Libya and with the Seventh Special Forces in Colombia. He says:

I was in Libya when they bombed [leader Muammar Qaddafi], and a year later, in 87, I was in the jungles fighting the Drug Lords in Operation Snow Cap. In Libya I was shot, in Colombia I was stabbed, and I was hit by the two I.E.D's in Iraq, but I was proud to be a soldier and I am proud to be an American Indian.

We are and have always been a vital asset to the military and other law enforcement agencies. Although we are still considered "injuns" and called "chief" and other derogatory names, we don't complain. We are still proud and we hold our heads up high as we have throughout history. But the fact that American Indians are fighting for this great country of ours needs to be recognized. We may have been a conquered people, but we were not a defeated people, and our warriors will always rise to the call of battle.

After the invocation, the American flag is lowered to half-mast. The announcer starts to call the names of the deceased society members, all military veterans. This is only my second time at the Kiowa Black Leggings ceremonial, and I don't know any of the veterans whose names are called. But as the announcer continues, I can't help feeling a bit emotional as I listen to the fate of each deceased veteran—the words "killed while in captivity," "killed in action," "body never recovered" send a chill through me. But the words that bring a lump to my throat are "forever 19 years of age" or "forever 21 years of age," reminding me just how young these Kiowa men were. As the list of deceased veterans is completed the flag is raised and the dance continues.

The Ton-Kon-Ga, or Kiowa Black Leggings ceremonial, is held in May and October at Indian City near Anadarko, Oklahoma. The Ton-Kon-Ga is an old military society founded in the days when the Kiowa fought other native nations for

At a Black Leggings ceremonial a woman dances in a dress of traditional black and red cloth and carries a lance.

hunting territory and fought the encroachment of the nonnative into their territory. Today, the Black Leggings Society honors the military service of its members. For a visitor attending the dance for the first time, it might seem unusual to see American flags and military insignias throughout the camp area, considering the historical treatment of the Kiowa by the U.S. government. Once young Kiowa men have enlisted into military service, though, the American flag and military insignias become an important symbol of their service.

Honoring the accomplishment of their warriors has long been a tradition among the Kiowa people. War deeds have been remembered through songs, painted on tepees, drawn in ledger books, and recorded on hide or muslin in the form of a calendar of events called a winter count.

One unusual tradition that has continued is the scalp and victory dances, which are done by the female family members of the veterans. The women dance wearing eagle-feather headdresses and carrying lances of their male relatives. This is an opportunity to appropriately salute the military accomplishments of the veterans, since it would not be considered proper for them to brag. The women also wear dresses made of red and black cloth, which symbolize the blood that was spilled in battle and the deaths that occurred. The passion displayed by the women is thrilling: Dancing vigorously, they shake their lances, while the voices of the singers mix with the trilling of the women's voices and the sound of the drum.

Once the women are finished, the male members of the society enter the dance arena singing unaccompanied. The members of the society are garbed in red capes, representing a captured war trophy from a battle with the Mexican army. Military patches displaying rank and branch of service are sewn to the capes. As they continue their entrance, the singers take over, accompanied by the drum. I don't have to understand the Kiowa words of the song to know how powerful it is.

In the Ton-Kon-Ga, there are two special positions held by young boys—Aw-Day-Tah-Lee (much honored son). As I read the account of the Aw-Day-Tah-Lee in the magazine *Whispering Wind* given by Vanessa Jennings, a Kiowa beadworker and cradleboard maker, I understood why these two positions were so highly respected by the Kiowa people. Vanessa says:

War bonnets adorn uniform jackets, an appropriate blending of two cultures and the warrior tradition that is so much a part of both worlds.

In one tribal memory, a group of Kiowas had gone on a raid. They ran into trouble and were cornered in an unexpected skirmish with battle-seasoned soldiers who had plenty of ammunition. The Kiowas were pinned down. If they stayed, they would all be killed. The decision was made by the leader to get the horses and make for freedom. The warriors had left their horses in the care of a quiet and attentive boy. The leader signaled for the

boy to bring all of the horses immediately. I can imagine the surprise of the soldiers when they saw this exquisite ten year old riding fearlessly into the middle of this fire fight leading the horses....The shouts and the bullets fell in a dangerous hail around that little boy as he held onto his mount and drove the horses past the soldiers and into the waiting hands of the Kiowas. I can see the tender care given that child's body as the Kiowas escaped. They made sure they did not leave him behind after that valiant act to save his fellow warriors.

—Emil Her Many Horses

AFTERWORD

My interest in telling the story of our nation's warriors in uniform began in 1972 when I interviewed Wolfrobe Hunt, a member of Acoma Pueblo, living in Tulsa, Oklahoma. He asked me to record certain Acoma sacred songs and prayers because he believed he was the last person who knew them and he wanted them preserved at the Smithsonian Institution so that one day members of the Acoma community could have access to them. He was worried these songs would be lost forever. I am pleased to say that after holding those recordings for more than 20 years they are now in the Acoma archives.

During these recording sessions, Wolfrobe sang the Acoma scalp song. I was surprised that the Acoma had such a song because the Pueblo people are noted for their pacifist ways. True, Wolfrobe said, but when necessary they could be fearless fighters and warriors and they had taken many scalps. When did the Acoma take their last scalp? I asked. Wolfrobe thought a minute and then said:

For sure it was during the Second World War. I know my uncle took a German scalp. It was in the closing days of the war. He was a soldier in the U.S. Army and he had been wounded during a fight to capture a German city. He was lying semiconscious in a gutter along a street when two German soldiers walked past him. One of the soldiers gave him a kick to make sure he was dead. The kick jolted him to full consciousness. When he realized what had happened, he was so angry that he rolled over and tossed a hand grenade at the two soldiers, killing them both. Then he crawled over and scalped the one he thought had kicked him.

Taking a scalp, Wolfrobe informed me, "carried responsibilities with it. The spirit of the person who had been scalped will always be hovering around, so my uncle had to take proper care of it. He had to feed it cornmeal and say the proper prayers so the spirit of the scalp owner did not harm him."

After hearing this story, I began asking other American Indian friends about their military experiences. One of those friends is Joseph Medicine Crow, who I met for the first time in 1973 when he came to the Smithsonian Institution to do research on his Crow people in the National Anthropological Archives. As director of the archives, I assisted him in his research and we struck up a friendship that led to his adopting me as his brother. From Joseph I learned about his grandfather White Man Runs Him and the other Crow scouts who assisted the U.S. Army during the Indian wars, and I heard of his own exploits during World War II, which earned him a chieftainship from his people.

The other key person in helping me tell the *Warriors in Uniform* story is Carson Walks Over Ice. I met him while visiting the Crow Fair in 1990. In a conversation with Mardel Plain Feather, I mentioned my interest in meeting Crow veterans for a possible book about Indians in the military. "Well," she said, "then you will want to talk to my nephew, Carson Walks Over Ice. He is a decorated veteran of the Vietnam War and his safe return was predicted in the Sun Dance. Everyone on the reservation knows that story."

BIBLIOGRAPHY

Ball, Eve. *In the Days of Victorio: Recollections of a Warm Springs Apache.* University of Arizona Press, 1970.

Benton, Kenneth L. "Warrior From West Point." *Soldiers Magazine,* February 1974.

Benzel, Lance. "Crow ceremony marks Marine's return from Iraq." *Billings Gazette,* April 12, 2006.

Bernstein, Alison R. *American Indians and World War II: Toward a New Era in Indian Affairs.* University of Oklahoma Press, 1991.

Britten, Thomas A. *American Indians in World War I: At War and at Home.* University of New Mexico Press, 1997.

Dippie, Brian W. *The Vanishing Indian: White Attitudes and U.S. Indian Policy.* Wesleyan University Press, 1982.

Dunlay, Thomas W. *Wolves for the Blue Soldiers: Indian Scouts and Auxiliaries with United States Army, 1860-90.* University of Nebraska Press, 1982.

Franco, Jere' Bishop. *Crossing the Pond: The Native American Effort in World War II.* University of North Texas Press, 1999.

Gibson, Daniel. "Desert Thunder: Powwow in Iraq." *Native Peoples Magazine,* March/April 2005.

Graman, Kevin. "Healing path from Vietnam a twisted trail." *Spokesman-Review,* June 25, 2005.

Hauptman, Laurence M. *Between Two Fires: American Indians in the Civil War.* University of New Mexico Press, 1997.

Healy, Donal T., and Peter J. Orenski. *Native American Flags.* University of Oklahoma Press, 2003.

Holm, Tom. *Strong Hearts, Wounded Souls: Native American Veterans of the Vietnam War.* University of Texas Press, 1996.

Langellier, John P. *American Indians in the U.S. Armed Forces, 1866-1945.* The G.I. Series: The Illustrated History of the American Soldier, His Uniform and His Equipment. Greenhill Books and Stackpole Books, 2000.

Linderer, Gary A. *Eyes of the Eagle: F Comany LRPs in Vietnam, 1968.* Ballantine Books, 1991.

Medicine Crow, Joseph. *Counting Coup: Becoming a Crow Chief on the Reservation and Beyond.* The National Geographic Society, 2006.

Nichols, Judy. "Native Americans Have Noteworthy War Record," *Arizona Republic,* March 23, 2003.

"Project Moccasins," *Native American Times,* April 19, 2995.

Roosevelt, Theodore. *The Winning of the West.* University of Nebraska Press, 1995.

Sheeler, Jim. "Wake for an Indian Warrior." *Rocky Mountain News,* January 21, 2006.

Tate, Michael L. "Soldiers of the Line: Apache Companies in the U.S. Army, 1891-1897. *Arizona and the West,* 16 (Winter 1974).

Townsend, Kenneth Williams. *World War II and the American Indian.* University of New Mexico Press, 2000.

Viola, Herman J. *After Columbus: The Smithsonian Chronicle of the North American Indians.* Smithsonian Institution Press, 1990.

White, Willliam B. *The Military and the Melting Pot: The American Army and Minority Groups, 1865-1894.* Ph.D. dissertation. University of Wisconsin, 1968.

ACKNOWLEDGMENTS

The author wishes to thank:

Brig. Gen. Gordon Sullivan, Association of the United States Army; Sgt. Chuck Boers, U.S. Army; Lt. Col. Mark A. Smith, U.S.M.A., West Point; Dr. Tim McCleary, Little Bighorn Community College; Chief Larry D. Nichols, Lower Muskogee/Creek Nation; Emil Her Many Horses, National Museum of the American Indian; Dr. George P. Horse Capture, National Museum of the American Indian; Dr. Joseph Medicine Crow, Crow Nation; Carson Walks Over Ice, Crow Nation; Toy Kelley; Nancy Tsoodle, Gary D. Kodaseet, and James D. Cates, Director, National Native American Veterans Association.

At National Geographic: Peggy Archambault; Barbara Brownell Grogan; Judith Klein; Olivier Picard; and Rob Waymouth.

CREDITS

2-3, Library of Congress; 4, Chuck Boers; 10-11, The Granger Collection, NY; 12, George Romney/The Bridgeman Art Library/Getty Images; 14, Herman J. Viola Collection; 15, Special Collections, Harvey A. Andruss Library/Bloomsburg University of Pennsylvania ; 16-17, Library of Congress; 19, Art Resource, NY; 20, Herman J. Viola Collection; 21, Library of Congress; 22, The Granger Collection, NY; 23, The Granger Collection, NY; 25, Courtesy of The North Carolina State Archives; 26-27, MPI/Getty Images; 29, Wisconsin Historical Society; 30, MPI/Getty Images; 31, National Archives and Records Administration; 32, Herman J. Viola Collection; 33, National Museum of the American Indian, Smithsonian Institution; 34-35, National Museum of the American Indian, Smithsonian Institution; 36, National Museum of the American Indian, Smithsonian Institution; 38, Denver Public Library, Western History Collection; 40-41, Library of Congress; 40-41, Library of Congress; 42, Library of Congress; 43, Edwin L. Wisherd; 44-45, The Picture Desk; 46, National Archives and Records Administration; 47, National Archives and Records Administration; 48-49, Courtesy Arizona Historical Society; 51, Library of Congress; 53, National Museum of the American Indian, Smithsonian Institution; 54, Denver Public Library, Western History Collection; 55, Library of Congress; 56, Milwaukee Public Museum; 57 (UP), Milwaukee Public Museum; 57 (LO), Milwaukee Public Museum; 58-59, Wisconsin Historical Society; 60, Indiana University Mathers Library Wanamaker Collection; 63, Oklahoma Historical Society; 64-65, Indiana University Mathers Library Wanamaker Collection; 66, Oklahoma Historical Society; 67, Western History Collections, University of Oklahoma Libraries; 68, Timothy McCleary; 69, Indiana University Mathers Library Wanamaker Collection; 70, Al Abrams; 72-73, CORBIS; 74, Courtesy Jon Malinowski; 75, Seely G. Mudd Library, Princeton University; 76-77, Joe Rosenthal/AP/Wide World Photos; 78, AP/Wide World Photos; 81, National Archives and Records Administration; 82-83, Seely G. Mudd Library, Princeton University; 84, U.S. Department of Defense/CNP/Getty Images; 85, National Archives and Records Administration; 86, National Archives and Records Administration; 87, Chuck Boers; 88-89, U.S. Army Signal Corps/AP/Wide World Photos; 90, Seely G. Mudd Library, Princeton University; 91, National Archives and Records Administration; 93, CORBIS; 94, CORBIS; 95, Seely G. Mudd Library, Princeton University; 96, Seely G. Mudd Library, Princeton University; 99, CORBIS; 101, Glen Swanson; 102-103, CORBIS; 104, AP/Wide World Photos; 106, National Archives and Records Administration; 107, National Archives and Records Administration; 109, 1st Lt. William Nichols/AP/Wide World Photos; 110, Courtesy Bonnie Stephenson; 111, CORBIS; 112-113, AP/Wide World Photos; 115, Official U. S. Navy Photograph courtesy of the Cherokee Heritage Center, Tahlequah, Oklahoma; 116, Courtesy Vernon Tsoodle; 118, The Harry S. Truman Presidential Library ; 121, Courtesy Vernon Tsoodle; 122-123, AP/Wide World Photos; 124, CORBIS; 126, The Minneapolis Institute of Arts; 127, Courtesy Teri Frazier; 128, Courtesy Vernon Tsoodle; 130-131, Herman J. Viola Collection; 133, National Museum of the American Indian, Smithsonian Institution; 134, Courtesy Vernon Tsoodle; 137 (UP), Herman J. Viola Collection; 137 (LO), Herman J. Viola Collection; 138-139, Military Times; 140, Chuck Boers; 143, Scott S. Warren/AURORA; 144-145, Chuck Boers; 146, Chuck Boers; 149, Chuck Boers; 150-151, Chuck Boers; 153, Chuck Boers; 154, Chuck Boers; 156-157, Chuck Boers; 158, Chuck Boers; 159, Chuck Boers; 160-161, Robert van der Hilst/CORBIS; 162, Chuck Boers; 165, National Museum of the American Indian, Smithsonian Institution; 166-167, Herman J. Viola Collection; 169, Herman J. Viola Collection; 170, Courtesy Linda Poolaw; 172-173, Todd Heisler/Rocky Mountain News/Polaris; 175, Courtesy Chris Lively; 176, Todd Heisler/*Rocky Mountain News*/Polaris; 178-179, Herman J. Viola Collection; 180, *Billings Gazette*; 182, Courtesy Emil Her Many Horses; 184, Courtesy Emil Her Many Horses.

INDEX

190

DEDICATION

THE WARRIOR SPIRIT

I close my eyes and all the noise around me fades…

I close my eyes and I am transported to another place…
home. The grass is lush green and the summer
breeze blows lightly on my face and the
smell of pine trees and happiness fill my nose…

I close my eyes and I can hear the drum beat in perfect
rhythm with my heart. The shrill cries of the
singers rise into the air and with every beat
my chest fills up with pride…

I close my eyes and I can see the warriors of my people
dance before me in such a way as to say, "We are
still here and we are strong…"

I close my eyes and I hear the voices of my ancestors
calling to me saying, "They could not put us down.
Despite every attempt they have made against us you stand
today… a YOUNG, STRONG, ANISHINABEKWE. Show
them the strength of the seventh fire. Your spirit is the
spirit of a million warriors, and no person or obstacle shall
put you down. We will always watch over you."

I close my eyes and grow stronger, even
for just a moment.

I close my eyes and I know… because I have the
strength of a nation beside me.

Alisha Schulman, Ojibwe
U.S. Military Academy, West Point
Class of 2009

WARRIORS IN UNIFORM

Published by the National Geographic Society

John M. Fahey, Jr., President and Chief Executive Officer
Gilbert M. Grosvenor, Chairman of the Board
Nina D. Hoffman, Executive Vice President;
    President, Book Publishing Group

Prepared by the Book Division

Kevin Mulroy, Senior Vice President and Publisher
Leah Bendavid-Val, Director of Photography
    Publishing and Illustrations
Marianne R. Koszorus, Director of Design

Barbara Brownell Grogan, Executive Editor
Elizabeth Newhouse, Director of Travel Publishing
Carl Mehler, Director of Maps

Staff for This Edition

Judith Klein, Project Editor
Robert Waymouth and Olivier Picard,
    Illustrations Editors
Peggy Archambault, Art Director
Rick Wain, Production Project Manager
Robert Waymouth, Illustrations Specialist
Nicole DiPatrizio, Design Assistant
Al Morrow, Production Assistant

Jennifer A. Thornton, Managing Editor
Gary Colbert, Production Director

Manufacturing and Quality Management

Christopher A. Liedel, Chief Financial Officer
Phillip L. Schlosser, Vice President
John T. Dunn, Technical Director
Chris Brown, Director
Maryclare Tracy, Manager
Nicole Elliott, Manager

Founded in 1888, the National Geographic Society is one of the largest nonprofit scientific and educational organizations in the world. It reaches more than 285 million people worldwide each month through its official journal, NATIONAL GEOGRAPHIC, and its four other magazines; the National Geographic Channel; television documentaries; radio programs; films; books; videos and DVDs; maps; and interactive media. National Geographic has funded more than 8,000 scientific research projects and supports an education program combating geographic illiteracy.

For more information, please call
1-800-NGS LINE (647-5463)
or write to the following address:

National Geographic Society
1145 17th Street N.W.
Washington, D.C. 20036-4688 U.S.A.

Visit us online at www.nationalgeographic.com

For information about special discounts
for bulk purchases, please contact
National Geographic Books Special Sales:
ngspecsales@ngs.org

For rights or permissions inquiries, please contact
National Geographic Books Subsidiary Rights:
ngbookrights@ngs.org

Library of Congress Cataloging-in-Publication Data
Viola, Herman J.
  Warriors in uniform / Herman J. Viola.
    p. cm.
Includes bibliographical references and index.
ISBN: 978-1-4262-0139-4 (regular)
ISBN: 978-1-4262-0140-0 (deluxe)
1. United States—Armed Forces—Indian troops—History.
2. Indian veterans—History. 3. United States—Armed Forces—
History. I. Title.
E98.M5V56 2007
355'00973—dc22
                                          2007028143
Printed in U.S.A.